"Simply outstanding. Matt deals with one of the most critical challenges in contemporary western Christianity: clarifying biblical, realistic priorities for our use of time. He gives a comprehensive, compelling template for sustainable Christian living. Pure class."

RICHARD COEKIN, Senior Pastor, Dundonald Church, London; Director of Co:Mission; author of *Ephesians For You*

"Make time to read this book! It is an easy read and full of amusing and relevant illustrations and useful ideas to consider. Full of biblical truth, it gives some firm challenges on how we spend our time. I've already made some changes."

LIEUTENANT-COLONEL JODY DAVIES MBE, The Royal Gurkha Rifles

"A great little book. Penetrating, engaging and realistic—make the time to read it, and it might just change the way you think about time."

CARRIE SANDOM, Associate Minister for Women and Pastoral Care, St John's, Tunbridge Wells, Kent, UK

"This is brilliant. If you're feeling time-poor, read it. It gives guidance not guilt, principles rather than rules, and freedom instead of burdens."

AL STEWART, Director of the Geneva Push; formerly Bishop of Wollongong, Sydney

"Time is a commore. Between work deadlines, ily, church activities—it seen ven fitting in the opportunity never once regretted taking th either will you, however busy you are. Thank you, Matt, for the wisdom and encouragement you have carefully crafted."

BARBARA LANE, Executive Vice President of LTI Inc., Atlanta

"In all of life's demands and duties, this book reminds you that there is only one essential activity—to listen to Jesus. A real gem!"

MARC DÖRING, Partner, Simmons & Simmons LLP international law firm

"If you are a busy Christian, I strongly recommend reading this book. It is wonderfully practical, and packed with careful biblical reflection and solid biblical wisdom."

WILLIAM TAYLOR, Rector of St Helen's Bishopsgate, London

"I am so glad I made time to read this book! How to make the most of limited time is an issue that faces us all. Matt's wise, clear and concise book (ideal for busy people!) shows us how the application of biblical principles can save us from wasting our time or burning ourselves out."

ALASDAIR PAINE, Senior Minister, St Andrew the Great, Cambridge, UK; author of *The First Chapters of Everything*

"This is a wonderful book that will help us to rethink and refocus. Matt reminds us that the time we have is God's gift to us to use wisely, without feeling burdened or guilty. The book is full of practical tips and real life examples that enable us to live godly lives under the pressures of work, church and family life."

ANDREW PERRY, Consultant Orthopaedic Surgeon

"Many Christians experience time as a pressure and a burden. Matt has drawn on his experience as senior pastor of a city-centre church to give us a thoughtful, warm, and tremendously practical book. It is realistic and grace-filled. Busy Christians will find this a challenging and encouraging stimulus to godliness."

CHRISTOPHER ASH, Director of the Cornhill Teaching Course, London; author of *Pure Joy* and *Zeal without Burnout.*

TIME FOR
EVERY THING?

MATT FULLER

thegoodbook
COMPANY

*To the many at Christ Church Mayfair who
constantly strive to serve the Lord with their time,
especially the elders and their wives.
I wrote this book for you in the first instance.
I hope it helps.*

Time for every thing? *How to be busy without feeling burdened*
© Matt Fuller/The Good Book Company, 2015. Reprinted 2016.

Published by
The Good Book Company
Tel (UK): 0333 123 0880
International: +44 (0) 208 942 0880
Email: info@thegoodbook.co.uk

Websites:
UK: www.thegoodbook.co.uk
North America: www.thegoodbook.com
Australia: www.thegoodbook.com.au
New Zealand: www.thegoodbook.co.nz

Unless indicated, all Scripture references are taken from the HOLY BIBLE,
NEW INTERNATIONAL VERSION. Copyright © 2011 Biblica, Inc.™
Used by permission.

ISBN: 9781910307823

Cover design by Jon Bradley at ninefootone creative

Printed in the UK

CONTENTS

1	The elusive gift of time	7
2	Why are we worn out and weighed down?	17
3	Time for rest	29
4	Time for trust	41
5	A waste of time?	49
6	Time for priorities	59
7	Time for work	71
8	Time for family	85
9	Time for church	99
10	Time for leisure	111
11	Time for resolutions	123
12	Time for bed	137
	Thank you...	142

1. THE ELUSIVE GIFT OF TIME

A few weeks ago my wife asked me what I wanted for my birthday. No doubt she expected the normal dull answers: a new pair of shorts, a tie, or something wild like some new glasses.

To her surprise, my instant, instinctive answer was:

Time.

Time. I would love to have more of it. I would love to feel less rushed and tired. I would love to sit in a chair and read a novel for a whole morning. I would love to sit and stare at the sea for an afternoon. I would like some time.

There are occasions when I look at my retired parents and in-laws with envy, because they seem to have time. Making a cup of coffee used to be something my dad did while juggling other tasks, but now that he's eighty it has become an event. He talks about doing it ten minutes in advance. Then he enjoys the creation and consumption of his cup of coffee before finally he reflects upon the fact that he enjoyed that cup of coffee. Sometimes I look upon that pace of life and it looks great! And yet, even retirees often feel that they don't have enough time. Everyone reaches the stage when they know that time is running out.

THE FAMINE OF TIME

Many of us feel a famine of time. We never have enough to accomplish all our goals and we are constantly dashing from one thing to the next. There's not enough time to ring a friend. There's not enough time to see the kids before they go to bed. Not enough time to read that book that I want to. Not enough time to have lunch away from the desk.

Maybe it was better when I was younger. But not according to those who are younger. Take the case of Martha Payne, the Scottish ten-year-old who became an internet sensation when her school tried to ban her from taking photographs of her school lunches and rating them on her blog. One of her complaints was: "There's not enough time to eat lunch ... I would like to sit in one seat for the whole of my lunch, but I keep getting moved on so tables can be cleaned." So young, yet so rushed!

Maybe it was better in the past then. Surely they can't have felt rushed 150 years ago. Yet it's not hard to track down precisely the same sentiment in those who lived and died in previous centuries. An historian called William Smith commented on changes to the Yorkshire town of Morley in 1886:

With the advent of cheap newspapers and superior means of locomotion ... the dreamy old days are over ... for men now live and think and work at express speed. They have their Mercury or Post laid on their breakfast table in the early morning and if they are too hurried to snatch from it the news during that meal, they carry it off to be sulkily read

as they travel, leaving them no time to talk with the friend
who may share the compartment with them. The hurry and
bustle of modern life lacks the quiet and repose of the period
when our forefathers, the day's work done, took their ease.

There were hardly high-speed railways with WIFI everywhere, and yet the same attitude was there. I wonder what William Smith would have made of newspapers being half-read at best before being discarded, or the volume of information provided by the internet, or the level of communication by email emoticons. But what his comments do reveal is that it has always been possible to feel rushed or harried. It is not a modern phenomenon; it is a struggle for humanity living in the world, rather than only for 21st-century people living in the modern world. Time has always been the gift everyone wanted, and very few people enjoyed.

Perhaps the problem is not with how much time we have, but with how we view it. Is the problem perhaps with us? Time famine is not a 21st-century phenomenon. Phrases such as: "Doesn't time fly" ... "Time marches on" ... "He's cash rich, time poor" have been around for a long time.

Still, we do have to recognise that the technological revolution has accelerated, and continues to accelerate, the pace of life. Most of us are never too far from a mobile phone or our emails. Many of us find it very difficult not to check our messages or log into Facebook on a regular basis. Some of us can't enjoy an event without spending it checking what others are doing at other events, or what's going on in the office.

How did life become so rushed? I always feel better if there's a convenient individual to blame. It's always satisfying to find a scapegoat. I've looked hard, and I've found one. His name is Peter Henlein. He is responsible for our battle with time. Why? Because in 1504, he invented the first pocket watch. Ever since then, we've been able to carry around with us a ticking measure of the day's disappearance. He caused the experience of glancing at our watches with despair, either because there is so much still to do in the remaining time, or because we know we have wasted a whole lot of time.

Since Peter Henlein isn't around to confront, I had to resort to asking my wife for the impossible: time. I live with the nagging knowledge that there simply isn't enough time. For me, time has become an enemy that I need to defeat and conquer. It has assumed the likeness of a crocodile that I try to wrestle to submission while it thrashes its tail and gives me the runaround.

On the other hand, for some of us it's not that 24 hours are too little; the problem is that they're too much. You may know the feeling of simply trying to fill your time. We're not in overdrive because we're not in gear at all. In the film *About a Boy*, the lead character played by Hugh Grant divides his day up into half-hour units because it's less intimidating trying to fill up a day that way. Taking a bath is one unit, or block; watching a TV quiz show is one unit; going to the hairdresser is four units. It's a caricature, but some of us can while away units on mindless TV or doing "research" on Facebook. Time is still an obstacle to be overcome. There is little pleasure or enjoyment in filling our time. Perhaps we're wasting a lot of it in the simple effort to fill it.

At the risk of stating the obvious: it's not meant to be that way. Time is not meant to be a tyrant because there's too much of it or too little. If time is a monster to me, then something has gone badly awry in my thinking! Hard work is good, and making the best use of time is good; but obsessing about time, being burdened by a lack of time, feeling guilty all the time, is bad. We know that, but how can we escape it? That's what this book is about.

We have actually been given a lot of time. Time is a gift—a gift we're designed to enjoy. The Bible would encourage us to see time not as a wretched commodity that we never have enough of, but as a gift.

Let me say that again—it's really important! Time is a gift to enjoy. There is, and will always be, 24 hours in a day. That won't change. What needs to change is how my heart views those hours.

THE MARCH OF TIME

Here's one view of time from the writer of the Old Testament book of Ecclesiastes. He's known as the "Teacher".

[1] There is a time for everything, and a season for every
activity under the heavens:

[2] a time to be born and a time to die,

a time to plant and a time to uproot,

[3] a time to kill and a time to heal,

a time to tear down and a time to build,

[4] a time to weep and a time to laugh,

a time to mourn and a time to dance,

[5] a time to scatter stones and a time to gather them,

a time to embrace and a time to refrain from embracing,

[6] a time to search and a time to give up,

a time to keep and a time to throw away,

[7] a time to tear and a time to mend,

a time to be silent and a time to speak,

[8] a time to love and a time to hate,

a time for war and a time for peace.

(Ecclesiastes 3 v 1-8)

Did you read that poem in both a negative way and a positive way? It's possible to do this negatively—you cannot resist the march of time; it is relentless and unstoppable. Yet the poem can also be read positively—God has designed a time for everything, so that we can enjoy the variety of experiences that this life has to offer. I think that the Teacher wants us to see both of these as true, but that the liberating response is to view time as the gift of God.

The most obvious point this poem makes is that we're not in charge of time. We do not decide when we are born or when we die. If we want to grow decent crops, we have to plant in autumn and uproot in the summer. If you are a shepherd, there is a time to heal an injured lamb and a time to cook and eat it. So the Teacher gives us 14 pairs of truths: each time, a negative and a positive, covering the natural life cycle (v 2-3); emotions (v 4); and activities (v 5-8). He wants us to recognise that we dance to a tune that is not of our own making and that we cannot alter. We cannot resist the seasons nor shift their order. Round the years go: another birthday; another Christmas; pull out the summer shorts; pull on the autumn layers; pull out the winter coats; another Christmas, and... repeat.

Yet it's not simply the seasons of the year that control us but the seasons of life. Some seasons are joyous: a wonderful holiday with friends; your wedding; and a newborn child. Others are tragic: the death of a stillborn baby; watching your parents' divorce; the death of a close friend. Life goes around and around and then there is a "time to die". Depressing, isn't it, to dwell upon life like that?! As the poem continues:

> 9 What do workers gain from their toil? 10 I have seen the burden God has laid on the human race. 11 He has made everything beautiful in its time. He has also set eternity

in the human heart; yet no one can fathom what God
has done from beginning to end. (3 v 9-11)

"Gain" (v 9) is a business word meaning "profit". If you're a shopkeeper, you make money by selling goods, you pay your suppliers and other costs, and whatever is left is your profit or gain. The Teacher is asking: *What profit will you have in life? What is the reward for your toil at work and at home? When you lie on your deathbed, what will you have to show for your brief time on this earth?*

Even here and now, doesn't it often feel that we are toiling just to keep our heads above water, or toiling to try and achieve something useful with our time? That's what the Teacher is describing here. My own experience has often been of feeling that I am disappointing people—I am failing to give enough time to people at work, to my immediate family, to my wider family, to my church and to my friends. There simply is not enough time to satisfy everything I want to do and everyone I want to please. There may be a time for everything that God expects, but there is not time for *every* thing that could be done. And that leads to the burden of "toil" without profit.

We know and experience wonderful, joyful moments in life that speak of something truly beautiful (v 11), yet they are tainted by frustration. Triumphs fade, holidays end, contentment passes and we are left with an endless "to-do" list and the feeling that we are letting people down again. Even some of those who have achieved greatness are uncertain of what they've really achieved. Back in the summer of 2012, Bradley Wiggins won the Tour de France and then Olympic gold. When interviewed after receiving his medal, he commented: "There was a light melancholy on the podium; nothing will ever top this." That's the burden of time; even the great moments pass.

THE GIFT OF TIME

So far, so glum. But then the Teacher says something that can transform our thinking:

> [God] has made everything beautiful in its time. He has also set eternity in the human heart; yet no one can fathom what God has done from beginning to end. (v 11)

The Christian knows that we can trust in the plan of God: that he has made everything beautiful in its time. The word translated "beautiful" here is a visual term used for physical beauty. The Teacher is saying that God's rule over time is staggeringly beautiful. It takes your breath away and makes you look twice, even though we may often only see a glimpse of it.

Yet at the same time, God has set both frustration and beauty into this world so that we look beyond this world and to him in order to enjoy the glory without the irritation. God "has also set eternity in the human heart". When we feel as though life does not offer enough time, it's because we were made for something more. We were designed to enjoy an eternity of time. If we accomplish everything we dreamed of in this life, it's likely our dreams were too little.

But, though we sense we need more time, "no one can fathom what God has done". We struggle to remember that we are not in charge of time. We need rescuing from the illusion that we can decide upon the times for laughter and dancing; we need to abandon any pretence that we can control life in this world, and to give up the thought that we are able to find the time to do everything that we desire. If we believe that we are in control, it will only produce frustration and bitterness.

We cannot master the seasons of life but we can trust the Lord who does! Knowing this is the key to viewing time as God's gift.

What kind of life does this lead to?

> [12] I know that there is nothing better for people than to be happy and to do good while they live. [13] That each of them may eat and drink, and find satisfaction in all their toil—this is the gift of God. [14] I know that everything God does will endure for ever; nothing can be added to it and nothing taken from it. God does it so that people will fear him. (3 v 12-14)

Wouldn't it be great to find that sort of satisfaction in our toil? Wouldn't it be lovely to wake each day with the thought: *God has given me time to enjoy and serve him with today and I'm looking forward to that?*

How wonderful to begin each day knowing that your day has purpose, yet is manageable—that you will be busy, but not feel burdened by it. How lovely it would be to end each day tired but not exhausted; satisfied, rather than anxious; and fulfilled, rather than guilty—to know there is a time for everything that God expects, but not time for *every* thing that could be done; and to feel OK about that.

That's the gift of God—and that's what we're exploring in these chapters. So in the first half of the book we'll be laying some foundations in terms of how we view time, busyness, and burdens; and then in the second half we'll look at how to use our time well (and avoid using it badly) in the areas of work, family, church and leisure.

And I'll be trying to keep each chapter short, because... we're short of time!

2. WHY ARE WE WORN OUT AND WEIGHED DOWN?

"Stressed office workers in China are paying to scream abuse at a stranger."

I read this recently in a newspaper article. A service has been set up called "Curse Absorber", where you can ring up and scream out all of your pent-up anger to a stranger at the end of a phone-line. You can either pay £2 for a five-minute rant with minimal response, or £3 if you want someone to argue back at you.

I was slightly frustrated that the article didn't provide the phone number (though I didn't have time to ring anyway). But I reckon that if you have got to the point where you find yourself dialling a stranger and paying to shout abuse at them, then something in your life really has gone wrong.

Most of us avoid getting that wound up, but we are frequently ground down by the busyness of life and the strains upon us. We don't snap at a stranger on the phone; no, we choose a stranger on the train, or our spouse at home.

There is a relentless stream of articles in the media about

"The exhaustion of modern life" or "Why we are all so tired". There is even a group now who have been labelled T.I.R.E.Ds They are the Thirty-something Independent Radical Educated Drop-outs. These are people who get to the mid-thirties, declare themselves exhausted, and quit their jobs. People can't even wait until mid-life to have a mid-life crisis any more.

Most of us are not quite at the point of burnout or dropout, but many of us will have moments of feeling that we're exhausted, zonked out, on our knees, and desperately needing some time out. We may not be T.I.R.E.Ds, but we're tired—and we're getting irritable with the demands that people are making of us or that we're making of ourselves. (I'm not talking here about struggling with medical conditions, but rather the tiredness that comes from having too much to do.)

If you have ever felt that the juice has been squeezed out of you and all that's left is a dry rind, then you need to hear, or hear again, some wonderful words from Jesus:

> Come to me, all you who are weary and burdened, and I
> will give you rest. (Matthew 11 v 28)

The offer is a wonderful one: rest. And what's just as wonderful is who the audience is. I love the understanding in Jesus' words. He makes the offer to people who are "weary and burdened".

Jesus knows well what it is to be wearied by significant burden. He knew physical tiredness (John 4 v 6). He knew the burden of having no opportunity to rest due to caring for others (Mark 6 v 31). He knew the exhaustion of conflict and the need to withdraw and regroup (Matt 12 v 15; 14 v 13; 15 v 21). The wonderful thing about God is that he is not a distant divinity floating above the clouds; in the person of Jesus, he came to live with us. And he did that not only so that we could understand that he is real, but so that we could know that he really understands.

It is with the utmost sympathy and gentleness that Jesus addresses those of us who feel over-stretched and over-tired. We'll think about the wonderful offer of rest in the next chapter, but before then we need to think about why it is that we are so often so weary and burdened.

OUT OF STEAM AND BURDENED DOWN

According to Jesus in Matthew 11, there are two related problems that feed into our exhaustion. We are...

1. weary, and...
2. burdened.

In the original text, the Greek word for "weary" is a "present active" verb—in other words, it is caused by things we keep on doing that exhaust us. It is an ongoing condition, and one that at the end of the day is our own fault. Weariness comes through our own relentless activity. It's the feeling behind the saying: "I've run out of steam".

The word for "burdened" is a "perfect passive" verb—caused by things that have been dumped upon us. At some point in your life a load was placed upon your back that you now live with. We may not have chosen to have these loads, but we have some choice over whether to live with them or remove them. The picture Jesus gives is of someone going about their day at work, or at home with the kids, with a bag of cement on each shoulder. Over time these really start to wear you down. They are crushing, and life becomes really hard work.

That's how these two problems are related. We tire ourselves out with activity, trying to overcome the burdens that have been placed upon us. We run out of steam because we're living life overloaded. And while all of us are weighed down with different burdens, there are many that are not so dissimilar from each other. Read through these five burdens and see if you can recognise any of them upon your back.

1. BURDENED BY RELIGIOUS RULES

Elsewhere in Matthew's Gospel, Jesus explains the sort of burden that was probably foremost in his mind as he made this offer of rest for the weary. When speaking of the Pharisees, a group of religious leaders, he says this of their teaching:

> They tie up heavy, cumbersome loads and put them on other people's shoulders, but they themselves are not willing to lift a finger to move them. (23 v 4)

The Pharisees of Jesus' day placed an intolerable burden upon people. *Want to be a follower of God?* they asked. *Then you must keep all of these 613 rules that we have identified.*

I've seen this weariness first hand. When I was in my early twenties, I lived with three other guys, one of whom was a non-religious Jewish lad called Josh. He was full of life with an infectious laugh. One summer he visited Israel and came back resolved to live as a fully Orthodox Jew. It was really sad to watch the transformation in him. His clothes, hair and food all changed quickly. Within a couple of months he could no longer eat in our house and eventually he cut himself off from his old friends. He became incredibly intense and humourless. His particular branch of Judaism emphasised that when these Jews' good behaviour outweighed their bad, the Messiah—God's promised, chosen, saving King—would come. Now that's quite a burden to feel upon you! *If only I behave well enough, the Messiah will come.*

This is the primary sense in which Jesus refers to being burdened. It's the idea that you have to achieve your salvation through obedience to rules. The Bible would describe it as justification by works: I can justify my place in God's heaven by what I do. Not many are as extreme as my friend Josh, yet they do still feel that they must live up to a certain pass mark to be "good enough", to be accepted by God. In fact that belief lurks in many of us.

There have been times at our church where individuals have exhausted themselves in serving others, and have then resentfully collapsed for months. Upon reflection they would admit that somewhere in their thinking was the belief that they needed to earn God's pleasure through incessant activity. Spiritually, that will crush you. If you think that you must earn salvation, then unless you lie to yourself about how you're doing, you'll be exhausted or give up trying.

And yet there is something attractive about the exhaustion of keeping religious rules. The appeal is that salvation rests in my own hands. I'm in control of it. If I have to keep 613 rules or 10 commandments in order to be accepted by God, and I think that I have done so, then God owes me blessing now and heaven later, right? I've won, and I've achieved it myself. Some people treat religious activity much like running a marathon—a challenge that will take up a lot of time, but is very satisfying when you complete your goal! A former neighbour of ours used to go to a local church every week and complain bitterly about how poor it was. We asked her why she went and she replied: "I want to know that I've ticked every box on God's application form."

This is a theme that we'll have to return to a few times in this book—the desire for control. That desire lies behind many of our wearying activities. In different ways and from different angles, it is perhaps the burden behind many other burdens. It's the belief that: "I can do it. I want to achieve in my own strength out of my own resources. I'm not comfortable with trusting God alone."

Even at this stage, let's name this attitude for what it is so that we're not deceived: it's sin. A refusal to trust God and his good provision for us and those we love is a sinful longing for independence and control. It's offensive to God because it denies that we are dependent on him—that he is God, and we're not—and it will crush us as we try to take on too many burdens that are not ours to carry.

There is some appeal in thinking that you can earn salvation. It allows you to remain in the driving seat, to be in control. Yet it's a terrible burden that will leave you exhausted and bitter, because it is impossible to achieve. Even worse, it's a burden that will leave you outside heaven, because entry is based on asking for an undeserved place, rather than offering our good deeds or religious rule-keeping as though we deserve it.

2. BURDENED BY A NEED TO "PROVE MYSELF"

The non-religious cousin of being burdened by religion is being burdened by the need to prove myself. Both can use the same language of justification. We want to "justify ourselves"—that is, we want to show that we should be taken seriously, respected and listened to. Many of us live life driven to achieve something so that we will impress people. The self-imposed burden of "striving to achieve respect" is particularly dangerous in driving our use of time.

The Oscar-winning actress Dame Helen Mirren has had an extraordinary career and has probably reached the indefinable level of "national treasure". Yet she's honest enough to reveal what drives her, even after all her success:

> *I wake up in the morning sometimes wanting to retire from my own ambition. Let me go, I say, let me go. Please let me go! Haven't I done enough? Proved myself enough to myself? Can't I be left in peace now? Why am I still eaten up with envy at what everyone else is doing? Why always the continuous anxiety, the worry, the one eye over the shoulder, wondering what's around, worrying who's being offered what? God, I wish I wasn't like that. I'd give anything to know what satisfaction feels like.*

I don't think she's unique; I think she's just honest. The burden of proving ourselves either to others or ourselves is a massive driver in many lives. And it's exhausting, because nothing we do or gain is ever enough.

A friend of mine works for a divorced boss. It was an acrimonious split and he rarely sees his children. Now he channels all of his energy into work and is incredibly driven to succeed there. You don't need to be any kind of psychologist to see that he is desperate to achieve in one arena of life, to make the sacrifice of his family on the altar of career worthwhile. His family life is a mess and so now he is determined to achieve in his professional life. He feels that he MUST succeed in his professional life in order to have something to show for his life. If things go badly at work, he rages. If things go well, it's never quite enough. That is exhausting.

3. BURDENED BY EXPECTATIONS OF OTHERS

A close relative of "proving myself" is being driven to meet the expectations of others.

The former England soccer manager Fabio Capello used to suggest that the England soccer shirt was very heavy—the players felt a pressure of expectation and so played badly.

My own soccer skills have been continually overlooked by the English football management, so that's not a burden that I've faced. Yet there are many other "burdens of expectation" that others, either consciously or subconsciously, place on us.

Sometimes these expectations can come from parents. They may want us to do better than them or emulate their success. We may know that they have made all sorts of sacrifices to help us and so we feel the burden of not letting them down.

When I was a schoolteacher, I taught a lovely lad called Ted. His parents were both high-flyers in their jobs. His grandfather, father and older brother had all gone to the same college at Cambridge University and the expectation was that he would do the same. However, he was a different sort of boy with different qualities from his brother. When I suggested as much to his parents, they tore my head off. It was very painful to watch him in his last year at school go from a very happy guy to an insecure wreck. He flunked his exams and then bummed around for a year doing nothing. He had been crushed by the expectations upon him. He's not that rare. Not many parents would weigh their kids down with bags of cement to carry all day; yet it is possible to unwittingly weigh down our children with expectations that are just too heavy for them and will distort their young hearts.

Of course, it does not have to be parents. It could be a spouse, a well-intentioned friend or a boss at work. Part two of this book looks at the genuine biblical demands placed upon us in our different relationships; but often we are wearying ourselves because the expectations we feel placed upon us by others are more than we can bear, and more than God asks.

4. BURDENED BY THE NEEDS OF OTHERS

It's very easy to pick up this burden, particularly if you're a Christian. We're told to love one another in a sacrificial and costly way. However, while serving others is costly, it's not meant to be crushing. Sacrifice in the Christian life is normally meant to be sustainable over a lifetime. It's a lifestyle of sacrifice rather than dying young. Sometimes we make caring for others burdensome by feeling that too much rests upon us: "If I don't help them, who will? If I don't show them Christ, they'll never find him." At other times, people expect unreasonable amounts of our time and emotional involvement. It's hard to know when it's right to give of ourselves, and when to say no.

I used to work with a man who would sometimes say to me: "Take off your 'hero cape' and tuck your pants in!" It was his way of mockingly saying to me: *You are not Superman and you cannot help everyone.*

Some people take on the burdens of others because they love to feel needed. Carrying the burdens of others can generate an over-inflated sense of purpose and importance. The motive for helping others might not be love for others but self-fulfilment. It can be hard to spot in ourselves, because it seems to be loving. Yet if we become angered when people no longer seem to need us, or when people turn to someone else instead of us, then our motive was probably wrong.

Some take on the burdens of others because they worry obsessively about what people think of them and they long to be liked. They cannot say "no". This one feels a little close to the bone for me. A typical scenario is when a guy at church asks to meet me on a midweek evening. I say "yes" even though I have no time, and then I walk away from the conversation irritated with them for not understanding how busy I am. Why not simply say "no" politely to begin with? Because I sometimes have an unhealthy care for the opinions of others. The brutal truth I need to tell myself is that caring for others in order to make them like me more or to impress people is not love—it's manipulation.

We can help bear the burdens of some people for some periods of time. Yet when we think that too many people need us, then we are throwing too many cement bags on our shoulders. Eventually we'll collapse. I know.

So, if you find yourself often thinking: "No one else can do this except me" it may be that you've placed yourself in the role of God. He doesn't need you to do that. He has run the whole cosmos for a long time. He can manage without you.

5. BURDENED BY TRYING TO BE SECURE

Some of us obsess about being "safe". We think that if we remain on top of circumstances, then we'll be secure: "If I can just have £x in the bank, then I'm secure and the future is safe". "If I can just get my child into that school, then their future will be secure." "If I go to work an hour earlier than normal this week, then I'll be securely in control." The problem is that all of these tasks can be bottomless pits. If we're seeking security in life, not only are we carrying bags of cement on our shoulders, we're trying to do so while walking up a down escalator. Life is too complicated and unpredictable for us ever to truly feel as if we're in control and secure.

The US President Dwight Eisenhower once said:

> *If you want to be totally secure go to prison. You're guaranteed food, clothing, medical care and all you need. There is a downside though...*

Attempting to make ourselves secure is its own prison, emotionally. There is always more that we could do and more that we could worry about. It is, again, a burden that will drive us to weariness.

HELP!

We haven't yet even considered "short-term crises" and what impact they have on our time—a dying relative or a family crisis can blow all of our time-keeping out of the water. There are what we might call emergency time pressures, which are a great drain upon our time and our physical and emotional energy.

However, while Jesus cares about all of our anxieties, his offer in Matthew 11 is to those who have wearied themselves with long-term burdens—not the sort that pass quickly when the immediate circumstances change, but the ones that we carry for months, years, or a lifetime. He's talking about the burden of religious rules and all the secular cousins of that problem.

So how many of the five burdens we've identified in this chapter do you recognise in yourself?

If you feel weary and worn down, at some point you need to sit down and work out why. You need to begin on your own, and then ask others to help you discern what are the presenting crises of life that will pass, and then what are long-term burdens that you need to address.

It's not actually that hard to work out the burdens you carry. Ask yourself:

- *What do I lie awake at night thinking about?*
- *When do I get most angry or worried? What is in jeopardy that arouses those feelings? Who is it that makes me feel that way?*

Feeling burdened is not inevitable. Feeling burdened is actually a sign that something is wrong in our view of life, because there is something wrong in our view of God. Jesus calls us to come to him, so that we can know satisfaction instead of feeling shattered. As Helen Mirren puts it, so eloquently but sadly:

> *Why always the continuous anxiety? God, I wish I wasn't like that. I'd give anything to know what satisfaction feels like.*

If only the second sentence in that quote really was a prayer. If only she knew that there is one who says to her:

> "Come to me ... and I will give you rest."

3. TIME FOR REST

Everywhere I go at the moment, I see the same advert. Whether on the side of buses or inside newspapers, it's the same thing:

Tired of being tired? Get your energy back with Floradix.

Is it really that simple? One gulp of an iron-based syrup called Floradix and I'll be like Popeye after eating spinach, full of energy and ready to go? Maybe not. I need something more significant, and so do you.

Come to me, all you who are weary and burdened, and I will give you rest. (Matthew 11 v 28)

In the last chapter we identified some of the burdens that weary us. Now we're going to look at what precisely Jesus is offering, and how we can get it. On one level the offer is obvious: "rest". Yet when we hear that, we naturally think of stopping work: of taking time to recover or be refreshed. We'll see later that there is a "time to veg out". But here, Jesus is talking about a "rest" that is more significant. It's not just a night in with a good meal and good TV. It is rest for the soul—rest in life, not rest from life.

THE SHADOW OF REST

If we're to understand the offer, we need to do a mini tour of what the Bible says. The Old Testament has shadows of what Jesus offers. Essentially, God commanded a *time of rest* and promised a *place of rest*. Both of these find their fulfilment in Jesus' offer.

A TIME OF REST

In Exodus 20, once God had rescued his people from slavery in Egypt, he gave them the Ten Commandments, one of which was to "Remember the Sabbath day by keeping it holy". The purpose of this day of rest was that they could have a "sacred assembly" together and honour him (Leviticus 23 v 3). Everyone was to stop their regular work in order to be refreshed, and to have time to gather together to remember that God was their Creator. So "even during the ploughing season and harvest" they had to stop work on the Sabbath in order to acknowledge that God was the primary source of their food, and not their own labours (Exodus 34 v 21).

This command was expanded further in Deuteronomy 5. There, the people were told that they should not slave seven days a week, because they were no longer slaves! The Sabbath was a day to remember the Lord's work of freeing them from slavery in Egypt.

As well as the weekly day of rest for the people, the land they lived in was also to have a rest one year in seven (Leviticus 25 v 1-7). The point is the same: to teach the Israelites that the land belonged to God and they were completely dependent upon him—that they must live God-reliant lives, not self-reliant ones. God insisted upon a time of rest so that his people would remember he was their Creator, give thanks to him as their Rescuer, and trust his promises to provide for them.

A PLACE OF REST

Once the Israelites had left the land of slavery in Egypt, they headed for the land of Canaan. The Lord repeatedly promised that this land would be a place of "rest" (Deuteronomy 12 v 10; 25 v 19; Joshua 1 v 13; 21 v 44).

What did this mean? First, it meant rest from their journeying. All of us love arriving home after a long journey, especially if it is after a delay on the roads or at the airport. Arriving in the promised land after a 40-year delay in the desert must have been a great relief!

But "rest" means more than that. Rest also meant rest from danger and hostility:

> You will cross the Jordan and settle in the land the LORD
> your God is giving you as an inheritance, and he will give
> you rest from all your enemies around you so that you
> will live in safety. (Deuteronomy 12 v 10)

How wonderful! They would have no fear of enemies and so could enjoy all that they produced and achieved. Rest in the land was not relaxing inactivity, but rather productive activity that was not jeopardised in any way. God promised and delivered a place of rest where his people could receive their inheritance and work constructively without anxiety and fear.

With that Old Testament background in mind, let's turn back to Matthew 11 to see more clearly what Jesus is offering.

²⁸ Come to me, all you who are weary and burdened, and I will give you rest. ²⁹ Take my yoke upon you and learn from me, for I am gentle and humble in heart, and you will find rest for your souls. ³⁰ For my yoke is easy and my burden is light. (v 28-30)

Jesus' call is to do two things:

1. Throw our burdens upon him, by trusting him as our Saviour. He guarantees our entry into the promised rest of heaven in the future.
2. Take his yoke and learn from him, by obeying him as Lord.

Doing both—throwing and taking—is what gives us rest for the soul right now.

THROWING OUR BURDENS ON HIM

The New Testament promises believers a "place of rest" in the future and the "time of rest" which we enter now. These flow out of the shadows of rest in the Old Testament.

The place of rest finds its fulfilment in the new heavens and the new earth that God will restore in the future. That is the true promised land, which the Old Testament land of Canaan foreshadowed. That is where Christians will receive their inheritance and work in a place where there is no hostility—indeed no sin or frustration.

The "time of rest" is best thought of not as a single Sabbath day in the week so much as enjoying a "status of rest". In essence, resting in Jesus means giving thanks to him for saving us and trusting his promises to provide. Thoughtful Bible-believing Christians will disagree slightly on this, but it seems that the Sabbath is not primarily a day of the week; rather, it is a state of the soul (although that said, we will consider the wisdom of maintaining a weekly day off in chapter ten).

Fundamentally, to receive Jesus' rest now begins by laying down our self-reliance. This guarantees our entry into the land of rest in the future.

A few months ago I needed a large piece of wood to block up a door at home. The nearest timber merchant is only a ten-minute walk from our house, but I needed a sizeable bit of wood and so I drove there. Annoyingly, that day their circular saw was broken and the smallest sheet of wood I could buy was 8 foot by 5 foot. It wouldn't fit into the back of my car, but I wasn't to be defeated. "No problem," I said to the sceptical guy at the timber merchants: "It's only a ten-minute walk home. I'll carry it."

I'm not sure quite how much the plank of wood weighed, but I had to stop after about 100 metres and put it down. I started off by carrying it on my head but that soon hurt. Carrying it at my side was incredibly awkward and so I alternated between the two. After about 30 minutes, I had travelled about a quarter of the journey and I was feeling grumpy. My mood was not helped by various people walking past me and laughing at my plight. Others made helpful comments such as: "That looks heavy," or: "You need a lorry for that," and (as it started to rain): "That's an odd umbrella".

I had reached the point of abandoning my wood, or at least dropping it on the foot of the next person to make a "helpful" comment, when two guys crossed the road towards me and asked: "Where are you going with that? Let us carry it; you look knackered."

I was rescued. I walked; they carried. Within five minutes we were home.

In that feeble tale there is an echo of spiritual truth. Our pride means we sinfully rely on ourselves rather than on Jesus. I stupidly tried to carry something far too heavy. I would literally never have got home with it on my own. I could only reach home by letting someone else (or in this case, two someone else's—it was a very heavy piece of wood) carry it for me. When we try to carry the weight of living well enough to gain acceptance into heaven, we will do one of two things: we will give up, or we will be crushed. Either way, we won't make it. The world is full of people trying to be good enough and being exhausted by it, and it is full of people who have given up on the whole thing because they were exhausted by it.

Then Jesus comes up and says: *You look exhausted. Let me carry it.* When Jesus says: *Come to me for rest,* he is saying: *Abandon your sinful self-reliance. Let me carry the burden of your flaws—I'll bear their weight. I'll deal with them even though it costs my life. Let me get you home. I'll carry; you walk. In fact, no—I'll carry you. You just give it to me, and trust me.*

This affects everything! Once you come to Jesus and trust, really trust, that he has died for your sins and risen to give you new life, then your perspective on the burdens you find yourself carrying is utterly transformed...

EARNING SALVATION

Rather than being burdened by religious rules to achieve your salvation, you can know that Jesus has achieved salvation for you. Look at the cross: that's Jesus taking your sins and paying the cost of your rejection of God. Look at the empty tomb: that's Jesus rising to new life and offering you that same life. You can know with certainty that you will enter the promised land of heaven. So you can rest. You can look at your sins and say: *I'm no less accepted by God, all because of Jesus.* You're not crushed. You can look at your successes and say: *I'm no more accepted by God; it's only because of Jesus.* You're not proud.

And when we put down our proud desire to earn salvation, and trust that Jesus has achieved that for us, then this affects all the other burdens we carry.

Imagine a young man who decides to become a chef and open a restaurant. His wife is a bit nervous that he'll blow their savings and they'll be penniless. His parents tell him he's mad and it will fail. However, he goes for it.

He trains as a chef, buys a restaurant and hires the staff. He is determined that he will prove himself a success; he will provide for his wife and kids, and he'll show his parents, too.

It's a disaster!

His meals are OK, but they're not great. There's not enough trade; the reviews are poor; and his staff are morale killers. The young man stays later and later, working harder and harder. He becomes more and more stressed, panic descends upon him and his frantic efforts become increasingly manic. Things get tense with his wife. He never sees his kids. He stops ringing his parents.

Then, one day a well known celebrity chef walks into the restaurant. He has decided to take pity on the young man. He offers to come and personally run the kitchens and make the restaurant a wild success. He has used his contacts in the industry to turn the bad reviews to great ones. Even more, the chef has transferred one million pounds into the young man's account as a gift. It's done. Sorted. No strings attached. At a stroke, the young man is saved. His future is secure. The chef says to the young man: "I'll do it all. I'll pay off your debts and secure your future. Yet do stay and work alongside me. You can learn from me how to enjoy this job and you can keep the profits too."

Our young friend pauses for a moment... shouldn't he be relying on himself? But he's not a fool—he pauses only for a moment before thanking the chef from the bottom of his heart.

Yet the young man still has a choice about how he lives day by day. He may be saved, but he could still work manically as if the whole of the business rested upon him. He could toil anxiously, thinking that everything rests upon his efforts. He could still snap at his wife, fail to see his kids, and refuse to ring his parents.

Of course, this is not a perfect illustration. But it poses two questions:

1. If you've realised that you don't know your life is secure and your future is certain, will you listen to Jesus say to you: *I will sort it. No strings attached. Let me give you rest.* Will you stop relying on yourself, and start relying on Jesus? Maybe that's something you need to do right now—to thank Jesus from the bottom of your heart, give it all to him, and let him run your life.

2. If you know Jesus has rescued you, will you live like that? If you are a Christian, you have a daily choice to ask yourself: *Will I trust what Christ has done in the past and promised in the future, OR, will I still act as if everything rests upon me?*

Only if you fully embrace what Jesus has done to win your salvation—only if you live out your status as someone who is saved—will you be able to take off the other burdens that we've mentioned.

PROVING MYSELF

Rather than be driven by a need to "prove yourself", you can enjoy the truth that Jesus has provided a wonderful place and future for you. The living God himself knows you and loves you. That enables you to approach life with pleasure rather than with weariness. You are somebody already—an heir of Jesus' kingdom.

The resting Christian looks at the burden of proving himself and says: *I'm going to work today without the ambition to make a name for myself. My ambition now is to serve my God and do the best job I can for his glory. If I'm successful, then great. If not, the Lord knows that I've tried my best and that's okay. He still delights in me.*

ENSURING SECURITY

Rather than by being driven to constant activity to make yourself safe, you can relax, confident that Jesus has guaranteed your future rest. You are safe already. If you trust now the promise of God for future rest, then it will liberate you from frantic self-reliance and activity.

The resting Christian looks at the burden of ensuring they are secure and says: *God provides my security. I am never beyond his protection. I'll try to be wise in life, but ultimately I trust him.*

EXPECTATIONS OF OTHERS

Rather than being crushed by these, you can relax in the knowledge that Jesus' expectations are realistic. You don't need to live up to your parents' expectations of you, or anyone else's, but can confidently enjoy the fact that Jesus never asks more of you than you can do. You are accepted and approved of already.

The resting Christian looks at the burden of living for the approval of others and says: *The living God accepts me. If the rest of the world doesn't, I'll still survive.*

NEEDING TO BE NEEDED

Rather than thinking: *No one else can do this except me,* you can say: *I don't have the time to help Mr X or Miss Y. I can drop another commitment to help them, or find someone else to, or simply ask Jesus to, but I cannot and don't need to simply add them to my to-do list. The Lord will do what is needed.*

The resting Christian looks at the burden of feeling they alone can save the world and says: *Jesus, help me know who to help and who to let other people help. I entrust people to your care. I know it doesn't depend upon me.*

I often repeat to myself: "My past is redeemed, my future secure, so in the present I can rest".

Sometimes, I truly believe that—and life is much better!

TAKING HIS YOKE AND LEARNING FROM HIM

Rest sounds great, but Jesus didn't stop there:

> [28] ... I will give you rest. [29] Take my yoke upon you and learn from me, for I am gentle and humble in heart, and you will find rest for your souls. [30] For my yoke is easy and my burden is light. (Matthew 11 v 28-30)

Taking on a yoke instinctively feels less appealing. Yet, strange as it may sound, we need to realise that this yoke is good news too. Jesus is saying that there is work to be done, but he is offering to show us how to do life realistically.

Although we may have the status of rest now when we trust in Jesus, we will fail to enjoy rest for the soul unless we continue to learn from him.

The rest that Jesus offers is not merely withdrawal or time out from life, but a realistic pattern of living the whole of life. Rest is meant to be the writing that runs through the stick of rock that is the Christian life.

Time off is essential, but it can only provide temporary refreshment. Holidays are wonderful, but we have to return from them to real life. Jesus is offering a rest that affects everything. So, not only do we need to throw our burdens upon him (faith), we need to learn from him (obedience). We need to listen to his word and be shaped by him.

No doubt some of you reading this have been Christians for years and are thinking: *I'm a Christian... but life is still hectic, and I still feel under pressure.* Growing in God's rest takes time. When we come to Jesus and lay down our self-reliance, we enter his rest. Then we need to learn to appreciate this more and more. We need to embrace and absorb what Jesus has done in order for his rest to fully become our own.

In the second part of this book, we'll learn from him a realistic way of doing life. We'll look at all the different facets of life, and see how Jesus helps us to be busy without being burdened.

But you'll never be able to live like that if you haven't come to Jesus for rest (for salvation from earning your own eternal life, and from all the secular cousins) and if you're not prepared to let him teach you; if you're not willing to let him make some changes to you and for you. It's why no secular self-help book on time management can provide more than a temporary fix in this life, or anything at all beyond this life.

Jesus says: "Come to me ... Take my yoke ... and you will find rest for your souls." It's a promise. Not an unobtainable daydream. It's a promise. Even for you.

4. TIME FOR TRUST

Though I am in haste, I am never in a hurry because I never undertake more work than I can go through with calmness of spirit.

John Wesley

What do you think as you read that? Here's my first thought: *That sounds like a nice way of living—busy yet always with a calmness of spirit.* Here's my second: *It was alright for John Wesley; he lived in the 1700s. He didn't have to deal with hundreds of emails every week.* The only problem with my complaint is that it's estimated that John Wesley rode 250,000 miles, delivered more than 40,000 sermons, and gave away the equivalent of millions of pounds. He was "in haste" far more than I have ever been, and did far more than I ever will.

In this chapter we're going to look at how to be busy, yet calm. And the way to do it is to lead our lives in dependence upon the Lord, rather than living functionally in independence from him—to enjoy "trusting work" rather than enduring "anxious toil".

WHO BUILDS?

¹ Unless the LORD builds the house,
   the builders labour in vain.

Unless the LORD watches over the city,
   the guards stand watch in vain.
² In vain you rise early
   and stay up late,
toiling for food to eat—
   for he grants sleep to those he loves.

(Psalm 127 v 1-2)

Although he didn't always live by his own advice, Solomon—the smartest man the world had ever seen—wrote Psalm 127. He's very clear that trying to build a house, protect a city or build a family is absolute vanity unless the Lord does it. Either the Lord builds as we work, or we work without him and everything we build is useless.

For many of us, the blunt statement that "in vain you rise early and stay up late" may be quite a shock because we instinctively think that working harder is the way to build and to protect. Somewhere in our heads a little voice ticks away saying: "Want to build a career? Work harder! Want to build friendships? Socialise more! Want your investments to be safe? Rise early to watch them! Want to be popular? Go to bed late in order to check your Facebook status."

Too often, we are eating "the bread of anxious toil" (v 2, ESV). Rather than enjoying our efforts, we are fearful in them and our labours are driven by anxiety. We work super hard in the office or at home because we're scared of what will happen if we don't. Anxiety is democratic. You can be a 15-year-old, anxious to fit in at school, and so toiling away to be popular. You can be a university student, anxious about exam results, and so toiling away in revision. You can be in your late twenties, anxious about your career, and so toiling away to be noticed. You can be in your early forties, anxious about your kids, and so toiling away to get them to dozens of extra-curricular activities. You can be in your fifties, anxious about providing for retirement, and so toiling for the pension pot. There's always an opportunity for anxious toil! And it's very easy to excuse our anxiety while attacking someone else's. I could say to the 18-year-old: "What have you got to worry about? You've got no wife or kids to provide for." But I'm guessing the President of the United States could say: "Matt Fuller, what have you got to worry about? You want to know anxiety? Come look at my to-do list."

What is the antidote to anxious toil, at any age and stage? It's always and only in knowing that the living God will provide what we need. He is the one who builds and protects. He does not intend for us to bear ultimate responsibility for building and protecting. That's why he commands us to: "Cast all your anxiety on him because he cares for you" (1 Peter 5 v 7). You must not and need not live with anxious toil; the Lord has not wired you to survive and thrive that way. Cast it all upon the Lord.

In our family we're big fans of *House MD*. Every episode is basically the same—an incredibly complicated medical case that no one can solve except the sociopathic Gregory House. In one episode, a 17-year-old boy is admitted with a severe illness that no one can diagnose. Various treatments are tried but he gets worse. Eventually, House and his team discover that the boy's parents have recently died and he has been bringing up a younger sister and brother, fearful that if their parents' death becomes public, they'll be split up and placed into care homes. This guy is trying to study, to earn enough money to pay rent, to cook meals for his siblings and to bring them up well. The stress is literally killing him. He didn't need medication—he needed to give up responsibility that was beyond him.

In a poignant moment near the end of the episode, he's told by a sympathetic doctor: "You're not meant to have this responsibility. You should have a dad worrying about all this stuff."

God says much the same to Christians who are anxiously toiling. *You're not meant to have this responsibility.* And you *do* have a Father worrying about all this stuff. So cast your anxieties upon him.

BUSY EQUALS COOL?

It's not just the internal voice of anxiety that drives us to burn the candle at both ends. Another reason that we rise early and stay up late is that in modern, western culture, busy is cool.

Busyness has become a mark of success, and so in some circles—including church circles—you can be made to feel quite inferior if you're not frantically busy. "How are you?" we're asked. "Busy," we reply, and people nod approvingly. This is true of our working lives, family lives and social lives. We can begin to feel that if we're not manically busy, then we're missing out. As a young man told me recently: "If I've only got one function to go to on a Friday night, it does feel a little lame. It's far cooler to leave one early and arrive late at a second. It's good to pack in the social time." Is it?

Most commonly, peer pressure encourages us to toil anxiously at work. Overwork has become a badge of honour in some circles. Last month on the radio, I heard a young office worker in London say in an interview: "My boss would praise me for my hard work, and gradually my self esteem became dependent upon the judgment of my colleagues." If self esteem is tied to the hours you work, then you're in trouble! In the UK there are now numerous Workaholics Anonymous groups up and down the country. The Japanese term for workaholism is even more blunt—*karoshi*, which means "death by overwork".

Psalm 127 reminds us that anxiously stretching the hours in each day in order to do more is not inherently admirable. In fact, it's probably arrogant—driven by self-reliance or impressing others. It may be an attempt to achieve more than humans are designed to—an attempt to depend not upon the Lord but upon ourselves. It may be that we are much like the builders of the tower of Babel in Genesis 11, who built "so that [they] may make a name for [themselves]" rather than recognising that only God can confer greatness that lasts, and matters, and accepting that "unless the LORD builds ... the builders labour in vain".

In the film *Limitless*, the main character, Eddie, is a bit of a dreamer whose life will never add up to much. Then he begins to take the wonder drug NZT that enables his brain to run at 100% capacity rather than the normal 5% (the film's logic, not medical science's!). All of a sudden, he can knock off a novel in a night; he makes a fortune on the stock market; he can outwit criminals. I found the concept of a drug like that enormously appealing! I wanted to be like Eddie. Just imagine, I could have knocked this book off in one night rather than over the course of a couple of years. Wesley gave 40,000 sermons in his lifetime? Hah, I could do 400,000, while making a fortune on the stock market and funding gospel projects all over the world. I could be Billy Graham, Warren Buffett and Charles Dickens all rolled into one man!

Why is that so appealing to me? Because I'd love to achieve limitless amounts of useful things. Or to put it another way, I would prefer not to be a creature dependent upon God; I would love to achieve great things in my own strength. Ouch!

Psalm 127 reminds me, and you, that we are creatures. We do need to sleep. There is something profoundly humbling about that fact. It puts us in our place and reminds us that we are dependent. Don't feel guilty for pulling the odd all-nighter by way of revision or to hit a work deadline or just because you're out having fun. However, a lifestyle which is characterised by the feeling that "I haven't got time to go to sleep" is a refusal to trust God.

Sometimes I need to repent of what Hilary of Poitiers, way back in the 4th century, called "the blasphemous anxiety to do God's work for him".

THE DELIGHT OF TRUST-FILLED SLEEP

Restful, uninterrupted sleep is a beautiful thing. And it's a gift from God. The commentators are a little divided on the best way to translate the last clause of Psalm 127 v 2. It could be: "He grants sleep to those he loves" or: "While they sleep he provides for those he loves". Either way, it's great! More likely is the first translation, emphasising that we're dependent upon the Lord for one of the most basic of needs—sleep; and also that he is delighted to give it, and that it comes as we depend on him.

We are not to live by the mantra: "You snooze, you lose". God says: *You snooze, you win.* We know we need sleep, and feel more ourselves if we're getting it... yet I'm guessing that most people reading a book on this topic also know the misery of lying awake at night. We're tired, yet our brains are racing. At this point a simple prayer of: "I trust you, Lord. Amen", is not enough to send us off to sleep. I generally find in my own life that periods of sleeplessness come after a prolonged time of anxious toil or self-reliance. Like the proverbial frog in boiling water, anxiety has built up without me really noticing it until I have hit "boiling point" and I lie awake at night feeling STRESSED.

At this point, my lack of sleep is not because I have lost the Lord's love. It's because I have tried to build in vain. I have failed to trust him.

CHOOSING TRUST RATHER THAN ANXIETY

I know that life is not quite as simple as a choice between trust and anxiety. There are external pressures upon us sometimes that are hard to avoid.

For example, at our church we have a number of self-employed musicians. The pressure always to say "yes" to new work is enormous. Their capacity to say "no" to a demanding client is limited. In the early days of a business, there is wisdom in never declining the prospect of work, but the hope is that it becomes easier to say "no" over time. However, it's very easy for this kind of work to be driven by anxiety and fear. I think in this situation, as with every other, you have to decide to set some boundaries; otherwise boundaries will be imposed upon you. You need to have certain points in the week that are sacrosanct, and ask others to hold you to account.

However, while life can be complicated, the choice each morning is a simple one: anxious toil, or trusting work. I'm not talking about the odd all-nighter here or there, but which of those two characterises your life. We all make the choice, probably without noticing it, at the end of each day: either we will accept that we did what God gave us time for in that day and trust him for the things that were left undone, or we can reject his lordship and stay up all night, working or worrying or both, because everything rests upon our shoulders.

We also make another choice each morning. Either we begin the day with anxiety, get up and get going because, well, there's so much to do and so little time. Or we will begin the day in dependence upon God, listening to him and praying to him, because, well, there's a lot to do and we'll need his help. We'll walk into our day resolved to do what we can and to trust the Lord for the rest. We'll work hard and seek to make good decisions but remember that lasting success will only come if he is building.

Life is not as simple as prescribing eight hours sleep a day; nine hours work a day; five hours play a day, and so on. Life is complex. However there is a simple question to ask: *Am I going to live today in trust or anxiety? Will I live as though God is building, and I get to work for him; or as though I am the builder, and God gets to work for me?* One is a pleasure, the other a burden. One liberates, the other crushes. One gives sleep, the other keeps you awake.

5. A WASTE OF TIME?

On my calendar are but two dates: Today and That Day.

Martin Luther

All of us hate wasting time. The two-hour traffic jam. The meeting that is cancelled after we travelled to it. Sitting through a terrible film at the cinema. Ever thought to yourself: *Well, that's two hours of my life I'll never get back?* We hate wasting small periods of time!

But to waste our *lives?* That really is tragic.

We've just seen that God builds—we don't. Even more fundamentally, God saves us; we don't save ourselves. But then why bother doing anything? If God saves, then why bother serving? If God builds, then why bother working? If anxious toil is to be avoided, then why bother toiling at all?

The answer is that we were made to serve our God in ways that last into eternity. We were made to dislike wasting time, because we were given time so that we might use it.

I imagine that some people reading this book feel that life is very busy and they don't know how to fit everything in.

Others may be desiring a prod, because they know that they are idling away time.

But I think that most people are like me—capable of both extremes at the same time. I am able to feel as if I don't have enough time while also wasting my time. I am very good at frittering away time even while I am complaining that I need more of it.

TWO WAYS TO WASTE YOUR TIME

There are two ways in which you can waste your time. The first is by being idle or easily distracted. The most recent figures show that people in the UK watch television for 15.6 hours a week—that's 38% of their free time. In the US, the figures are even worse: 17 hours of television a week—41% of free time. And that's before we take social media into account. A church near us tried a two-week "fast" from all media in order to see how much time it freed up. They were stunned! Without the internet, TV and radio they "found" loads of free time. That may not be a practical way to live for 52 weeks a year, but it is striking how much time can dribble away without us really noticing. In one sense, we're busy doing things. But they're meaningless things. Filling our time with soaps, shopping and sofa-lounging busily sucks the meaning from life.

The second obvious way of wasting time is by being focused on and dedicated to the wrong things. It's easy to invest our lives in things that are fleeting rather than things that will last. I recently read a famous interview that Mohammed Ali gave just a few years ago. He was an extraordinary athlete. It is very hard not to warm to a man who smilingly declared before the "Rumble in the Jungle" in 1974:

I've done something new for this fight.
I wrestled with an alligator, I tussled with a whale;
handcuffed lightning, thrown thunder in jail;
Only last week, I hospitalized a brick;
I'm so mean I make medicine sick.

Yet in this interview, Gary Smith of *Sports Illustrated* visited Ali on his farm. They went into the barn where, on the floor, leaning against the walls, were paintings and photos of Ali in his prime: eyes keen, arms thrust up in triumph.

The reporter looked closer and noticed that across Ali's face in every picture were streaks of bird dung deposited by pigeons in the rafters. Silently, one by one, Ali turned all the pictures to the wall. Then, outside the barn, Ali stood motionless and muttered repeatedly:

I had the world and it wasn't nothing.

The life of Mohammed Ali is particularly poignant because the once great athlete is now ravaged by disease. Yet his words are telling: you can be the greatest, but it doesn't last. You can have the world, but it will pass. You can gain everything life has to offer, and have wasted your life.

We need to remember that each hour is a precious splinter of eternity that Jesus has loaned to us so that we might serve him. We can use each moment, and should use each moment, for him, in a manner that will last for ever. That's what Martin Luther was getting at with his quote: "On my calendar are but two dates: Today and That Day". We should live each day with a thought to the final day when Jesus returns.

In Matthew chapters 24 – 25, Jesus tells five parables to encourage us to keep watch for his return. Probably the most famous is the "parable of the talents" or "the parable of the bags of gold". It talks generally about the gifts God has given us, but it certainly applies to the gift of time, and it encourages and warns us that we should steward that precious gift carefully.

As with many parables, there is a "God figure"—the master—and then there is a positive example to follow and a negative one to avoid. Jesus is talking about the kingdom of heaven (25 v 1) and says it's like a man going on a journey...

JESUS ENTRUSTS US WITH SIGNIFICANT RESOURCES

> Again, it will be like a man going on a journey, who called his servants and entrusted his wealth to them. To one he gave five bags of gold, to another two bags, and to another one bag, each according to his ability. Then he went on his journey. (v 14-15)

In the parable, the master entrusts a fortune to his servants. Literally, the word Jesus uses here is "slaves". We are loved by Jesus and we are children of God; but we are also owned by Jesus, and his to command. We are here to do our master's bidding, not our own.

Each "bag of gold" is literally a unit of money called a "talent". This was 10,000 denarii, and a denarii was a decent day's wage. So a "talent", or "bag of gold", is worth somewhere over £1 million. The master gives £5,000,000, £2,000,000 and £1,000,000 to his three servants to invest and make good use of.

The point is that Jesus is not a begrudging master, treating us like children and so unwilling to give us £10 to spend on sweets. No, he gives us significant responsibility. I think that we're meant to understand this broadly. Our time, our money, and our abilities are all resources given to us by our master so that we might use them to grow his kingdom. He loans us all we have, and says: *Go and use these things to work for my kingdom.* Most pertinently for us, in this book, he loans us time and says: *Fill it in a way that grows my kingdom.*

PUT IT TO WORK

What we do with what Jesus gives us really matters:

> [16] The man who had received five bags of gold went at once and put his money to work and gained five bags more. [17] So also, the one with two bags of gold gained two more. [18] But the man who had received one bag went off, dug a hole in the ground and hid his master's money.
>
> [19] After a long time the master of those servants returned and settled accounts with them. [20] The man who had received five bags of gold brought the other five. "Master," he said, "you entrusted me with five bags of gold. See, I have gained five more."
>
> [21] His master replied, "Well done, good and faithful servant! You have been faithful with a few things; I will put you in charge of many things. Come and share your master's happiness!"
>
> [22] The man with two bags of gold also came. "Master," he said, "you entrusted me with two bags of gold: see, I have gained two more."
>
> [23] His master replied, "Well done, good and faithful servant! You have been faithful with a few things; I will put you in charge of many things. Come and share your master's happiness!" (v 16-23)

The two positive examples (we'll call them Mr Five and Mr Two) are commended for their activity. We're told that they "immediately" went and put their assets to work. By contrast, Mr One does very little.

We are meant to be busy! The Christian who knows that Jesus has given him gifts that can make an eternal difference, and who knows that Jesus will return one day, will be working hard. It is good to take some risks for the Lord. There is something wildly inappropriate in having small dreams when we are serving the King of the universe. There are times when I want a quiet life with no great effort and in which nothing much changes. I need reminding that an attitude like that would lead me to waste the precious gift of time that I have been asked to steward.

Recently, I read an interview with Frank Lampard, the England footballer who has won everything possible for his club and played over 100 times for his country. He recalled that at 16 he was viewed as an average talent with no great prospects. He wasn't one of the best 11 players in his age group at his local club. But every day he stayed later and trained harder, while the more talented players jeered at him as he practised in the rain. Twenty years later, no one knows their names; but Frank Lampard has gone on to be recognised as one of the best midfielders of his generation and has earned over £50,000,000 from his sport. He worked hard to make the most of the talent that he was given.

Jesus calls us to make the most of the time that we have been given by him, to be used for him. Christians know that we have a wonderful Master of a glorious kingdom and so we work hard, not for our own glory, but to maximise what we can do for his kingdom.

When the master returns, Mr Five receives the wonderful commendation: "Well done, good and faithful servant! You have been faithful with a few things; I will put you in charge of many things. Come and share your master's happiness!"

He is twice commended for his faithfulness. But what is "faithful" about him? It is his actions. He lived in a way that showed he knew the value of what he had been given, and the identity of the one who had given it to him. So for us, faithful living must mean using our abilities and our time and our opportunities as God-given assets to grow his kingdom. The reward is wonderful—it is the joy and the pleasure of serving the Master for ever in the kingdom to come. Just imagine seeing Jesus and hearing him say to *you*:

Well done, good and faithful servant.

I find it enormously comforting that Mr Two receives precisely the same commendation as Mr Five. We are not given the same opportunities and abilities as each other—but it doesn't matter. There are people in this life who are far more talented than me, with far greater resources than me and who will achieve far more for Christ than me. That's great! Jesus doesn't ask me to achieve the same as them. He asks me to faithfully use what he's given *me*.

There are some Christians that most of us have heard of. They have achieved great things for the kingdom of God. Yet there are also Christians locked up in North Korea who we have never heard of. It's unlikely that anyone will write a biography about them. They'll never write a bestseller or speak at a conference. Yet if they have used the limited opportunities they have to speak of Christ while living under a wicked regime, I expect that their "Well done" will be louder than yours or mine.

So, that's Mr Five and Mr Two. But then there's Mr One...

²⁴ Then the man who had received one bag of gold came. "Master," he said, "I knew that you are a hard

man, harvesting where you have not sown and gathering where you have not scattered seed. [25] So I was afraid and went out and hid your gold in the ground. See, here is what belongs to you."

[26] His master replied, "You wicked, lazy servant! So you knew that I harvest where I have not sown and gather where I have not scattered seed? [27] Well then, you should have put my money on deposit with the bankers, so that when I returned I would have received it back with interest.

[28] "So take the bag of gold from him and give it to the one who has ten bags. [29] For whoever has will be given more, and they will have an abundance. Whoever does not have, even what they have will be taken from them. [30] And throw that worthless servant outside, into the darkness, where there will be weeping and gnashing of teeth." (v 24-30)

This is not the book to unpack Jesus' verdict on Mr One. What we do need to see is that Mr One has a completely false view of the master. He describes him as "hard", which means he is "afraid". Jesus is describing someone who is not a Christian. They have a wrong view of Jesus, so they don't use what they have been given to serve him. The consistent message of the New Testament is that those who genuinely come to faith in Jesus stop living for themselves and stop holding God at arm's length, and joyfully live for him instead.

When it comes to our use of time, Jesus tells us here that we are slaves of a wonderful master, who calls us to maximise the time we have now in order to grow his kingdom. Your activity now will last into eternity and be rewarded with wonderful joy. I shouldn't have asked my wife for time; first, because she can't give it, but secondly, because I've already been given it! I've been given all the time I need to do what Jesus wants me to do (more on this later on). Jesus Christ is the magnificent King of the universe. He has given you time to live, and abilities to use. How daft that we fritter away our Master's gift of time on ourselves or on doing little when we could use our time to be used by him to build his kingdom.

A little while ago I watched a programme called *The Art of Dying*, which looked at whether art can be a comfort to people who know they're soon to die. As a part of the programme the BBC obituary writer wrote an obituary for the presenter, Dan Cruickshank. I thought his response was so striking that I watched it repeatedly on iPlayer until I had written it all down:

> *There were emotional ups and downs but, on balance, I can say it pretty successfully did the job of pricking my bubble of vanity. Is that a good thing? Probably... [it] does wake you up from the dreamy world of death denial—indeed acts as a* memento mori, *a reminder to strive in life and behave well before death is imminent. I've had a warning shot across my bow. I've been granted a glimpse of the future and have the possibility to use this knowledge and to redeem myself.*

It's an odd thing to be handed your obituary when you're still alive. I think that, for me, it would be a bit of a wake-up call. But what would you and I read if we could glimpse our heavenly obituary? Would it contain the words: "Well done, good and faithful servant"?

I became a Christian in my early twenties, while I was at university. Not long after, I was baptised, along with a few others. One of the guys was an older chap in his late fifties. We were all quite excited on the day, but after the service he came up to me and solemnly said words I shall never, ever forget:

I envy you. I wasted nearly sixty years of my life on meaningless things. How I wish that the Lord had saved me at twenty years old rather than at nearly sixty. God has given you time to serve him, young man. Don't waste it. Don't waste it!

6. TIME FOR PRIORITIES

"Everyone wants a piece of me."

That was my initial title for this book, until I was told that it was too negative. Yet, that is sometimes how I feel—there simply isn't enough time to do everything I want, or to satisfy the demands of different people. So, having considered what should and shouldn't drive our view and our use of time in Part One, we need to look more carefully at the competing demands upon our time. How do we plan our time so that we don't waste it? How do we go to bed content that we've achieved all that we need to and not feeling guilty? How do we find time for everything?

Well, the simple answer is: *we don't*. In any given week, there will normally be things on the to-do list that are not done. Accept it! There simply isn't the time to do everything that we desire. There really isn't time for *every* thing.

But there is time for everything God wants us to do. His to-do list does get done:

> For we are God's handiwork, created in Christ Jesus to do
> good works, which God prepared in advance for us to do.
>
> (Ephesians 2 v 10)

Can you see what an exhilarating and liberating truth this is?!
Before the creation of the world, God had certain works for
us to participate in, and tasks he expected us to do. He has
assigned activities for you and me to do so that we live lives
that matter; so that we undertake tasks that count. We're not
merely to meander through life, waiting to go to heaven; we
can purposefully fulfil the works that the Lord has given us.
That's great. And not only that—because it is God who has
assigned the works, we can be confident that he will give us
the strength and desire and time to perform them.

At the same time, we've seen already that he knows we're
creatures who need rest and sleep. He does not expect us to
stay awake 24/7 in order to fulfil all our commitments. Nor
does he give us so much to do that we need to do that. We will
not get to heaven and be rebuked for failing to work eight days
a week. The Lord knows what is possible for us. He desires us
to do the good works he planned for us, and he calls us to not
feel guilty over other good things which are left undone. He
calls us to do eternally significant things and equips us to do
them; but he does not demand that we do *every* thing.

Phew. But... what should we actually be doing? What does
God command us all to do?

Erm, actually, rather a lot! Among other things, we're to...

- *love and respect our spouses (Ephesians 5 v 33)*
- *honour our parents (Ephesians 6 v 2)*
- *bring up our children in the training of the Lord
  (Ephesians 6 v 4)*
- *obey our employers (Ephesians 6 v 5)*

- *pray continually (1 Thessalonians 5 v 17)*
- *practise hospitality (Hebrews 13 v 2)*
- *daily encourage church members (Hebrews 10 v 25)*
- *always be prepared to give an answer for the hope we have (1 Peter 3 v 15)*
- *be on our guard by reading the Scriptures (2 Peter 3 v 16-17)*
- *contend for the faith (Jude v 3)*
- *rejoice in the Lord always (Philippians 4 v 4)*

Even a cursory glance at this list makes it obvious that we can't be doing all of these things all of the time! So how do we plan our time? Here are some dead ends...

Some respond by ranking our commitments. On countless occasions, I've heard preachers say that God's priorities for our lives are ranked like this:

1. God
2. Spouse
3. Children
4. Church
5. Work.

My problem with this is that I simply can't see that ranking in the Bible! Why does "husbands love your wives" always trump "slaves obey your masters"? And how does it actually work in practice? If I have a 9-till-5 job, then what does saying my kids are more important than my job mean at 2pm on a Tuesday?

Another dead end is to be obsessive with time management, and try and allocate precise amounts of time to each area. Some people are very good at running their calendars to the minute, yet this can easily become an obsession. In Jonathan Swift's novel *Gulliver's Travels*, the author describes how the tiny Lilliputian people believe Gulliver's watch to be a god, because he never does anything without consulting it. Gulliver tells them that it points out the time for every action of his life. How boring! It is possible for time management to become an obsession—to become a god—and to have a concern with being productive that can border on slavery. By contrast, do you ever go on holiday and not wear a watch? It's fabulous. I feel an enormous sense of freedom when I'm asked: "What time is it?" and my answer is: "I don't know and I don't care because it doesn't matter!" Try it sometime!

SETTING SOME BOUNDARIES

So you'll find no ranking in this book, and no detailed scheduling either. The approach that we'll take is to look at several different arenas of life—work, church, family and leisure—and try to discern biblically what is the "floor to obedience". In other words, what should we do in that area of life in order to be faithful and obedient to God? This can help in two ways. The first is to stop us falling short and neglecting our God-given responsibilities. The second is that this is liberating! Plenty of voices will tell us what we "must do" at work or what we "must do" to be a good parent, or a good son or daughter, and so on. But, as long as we are fulfilling scriptural floor to obedience, then we are free to say "no".

At the other end, we need to work out what is an idolatrous obsession, where an area of life has become a god to us, which we worship and sacrifice ourselves or others for. There are fewer explicit passages of Scripture telling us when we have smashed the "ceiling of obedience" into an idolatrous concern with marriage or work or friendship. Often idolatry in one area is revealed by neglect in another. So, if I never commit to faithful service at church because it cuts into my supremely precious "family time", then idolatry of the latter has caused neglect of the former. Since God does not call us to obey him without giving us what is necessary to obey him, if we are not obeying him in one part of life, chances are we're being idolatrous in another.

When we've had a good go at establishing these "boundaries", then we can then consider good questions to ask of the area in between. God has given us great freedom in how we use his gift of time to us but there are few easy answers as to how we carve up our brief stay here on earth. Yet we need to consciously decide where we place boundaries on our use of time, or we will be at the mercy of others and boundaries will be imposed upon us. We need to know what we must do, what we we're free to say "no" to, and what we must not do.

Here's how it looks:

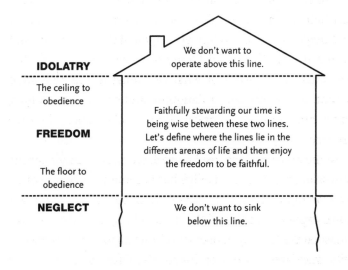

IDOLATRY

We don't want to operate above this line.

The ceiling to obedience

FREEDOM

Faithfully stewarding our time is being wise between these two lines. Let's define where the lines lie in the different arenas of life and then enjoy the freedom to be faithful.

The floor to obedience

NEGLECT

We don't want to sink below this line.

SO, WHAT DOES THE LORD EXPECT YOU TO DO?

Looking at our time in this way will not be as simple as "ranking" or "scheduling" approaches. But it will enable us to be more biblical in our approach; and since Jesus tells us how to live in the Bible, it will mean we're living under his yoke, his "light", liberating guidance.

Before we dive into more of the details in each arena of life, here are some points worth considering...

1. WE ARE TO SERVE THE LORD IN EVERY ARENA OF LIFE

"Whether you eat or drink or whatever you do, do it all for the glory of God" (1 Corinthians 10 v 31). I am a Christian. In every part of my life, that must define me more than anything else.

I am a Christian who happens to be a husband.

I am a Christian who happens to be a schoolteacher.

I am a Christian who happens to have two elderly parents still living.

I am a Christian who happens to lead a weekly Bible study.

I am a Christian.

All of the other activities will shape your schedule, but above all, you are a Christian. Whatever you're doing it must be for, and can be for, the glory of God.

We're not to view time as a pie that we cut up into a work piece, a family piece, a leisure piece and a God piece. It's all his—all of our activities are for him!

2. THE "IDEAL DIARY" DOESN'T EXIST

There are stages in our life where we may feel that we have everything in "balance". We are not rushed or harried, but serenely pass through each day. Those stages tend not to last!

There are other stages when everything seems constantly out of control. One of those is when children are pre-school age, careers seem to be at a crossroads and you seem to be on a dozen different serving rotas at church. This stage doesn't last either!

It's helpful to realise that whatever stage we're at in life, we need to pause and reflect on how we are stewarding God's gift of time to us. It may be we need to cut down and stop feeling guilty. It may be that we need to get busier and stop wasting time. It may be that, in different areas, both are necessary.

3. CHRISTIANS HAVE MORE COMMITMENTS THAN THEIR PEERS

Being a Christian is wonderful. But it does bring extra commitments because it brings an eternal purpose and a greater responsibilities. We need to spend time with the Lord, reading his word and in prayer. We are meant to be committed members of a church fellowship. These are not demands that non-Christian colleagues we know will have. Being generous in our financial giving will mean having less money available for holidays and leisure activities. The desire to be generous with money, or to buy a house in order to stay committed to our church, may create pressure for a family to have a second income.

This will raise difficult questions. For instance, if I have more responsibilities as a Christian than my non-Christian neighbour or colleague, will I:

a) simply be busier than them, with less time for leisure?
b) accept that I cannot compete in the office because I am unable to do the same hours that they do?
c) drop some other area of life, such as a hobby, sport and so on?

I'm not suggesting that there is one correct answer. It will vary for each of us. Yet we do need to be realistic and recognise the question. And we need to accept that we will sometimes look at friends, family or colleagues who aren't Christians, see what they do with their time, and wonder what we are doing with ours. The answer is (or should be): *I'm using my time for Jesus.* We need to remember that our time is really Jesus' time. We need to remember that we have already done the best thing with our time that we can—we have put our trust in Jesus, so that we never hear those dreadful words: "Depart from me" (Matthew 25 v 41). And we need to remember that we are using our time in a way that will mean we do hear those wonderful words from verses 21 and 23: "Well done, good and faithful servant".

4. WE NEED TO CHOOSE OUR ROLE MODELS CAREFULLY

Some Christians seem to cheat the dilemma I identified on the previous page by smuggling in another option:

d) Simply be more brilliant and receive more God-given talents than everyone else.

We need to remember that not all of us are "Mr Five". Some Christians are able to hold down a high-powered secular job, achieve phenomenal career success, raise a delightful family of ten children, win "spouse of the year" while caring for elderly parents, and hold evangelistic Bible studies in their home each week.

I am not that Christian. I am guessing you are not, either. If we try to emulate them, we will crush ourselves!

Sometimes role models can be helpfully inspiring. At other times they may simply feed our pride and drive us to attempt too much. Choose your role models carefully!

Remember that Jesus, the greatest role model you have, stopped to eat and stopped to sleep.

5. YOU CAN'T DO EVERYTHING YOU WANT

The list of activities that the Lord expects of us reveals one truth plainly and it's a really important one for this book:

We *cannot* do everything that we desire to do. We need to give up trying. But we *can* enjoy the time God has given us and usefully serve him.

It really is crucial to recognise that we cannot do everything that we desire to. Even Jesus couldn't:

> At daybreak, Jesus went out to a solitary place. The people were looking for him and when they came to where he was, they tried to keep him from leaving them. But he said, "I must proclaim the good news of the kingdom of God to the other towns also, because that is why I was sent." And he kept on preaching in the synagogues of Judea. (Luke 4 v 42-44)

There were many sick left unhealed; there were presumably many conversations not had. Yet at this moment, Jesus recognised that his priority was preaching—so that's what he did. Ultimately, he knew that his Father had sent him to die for our sins—so he left the crowds behind and walked to his lonely cross. We see Jesus walking away from conversations despite his sadness and walking away from the sick despite his compassion. He couldn't do everything he desired to; and neither can we. He did do what he was called to do; and so can we.

6. WE NEED TO PRAY FOR WISDOM

> If any of you lacks wisdom, you should ask God, who gives generously to all without finding fault, and it will be given to you. (James 1 v 5)

Working out the best way of stewarding our time is hard. It requires biblical input; it requires good counsel from others. Above all, it requires wisdom, so we must pray. Let me encourage you to do just that as you read the next few chapters, and think about how best to steward your time. You'll hopefully find yourself thinking about your own life and even making changes as you read each of the next four chapters—but when we get to chapter 11, we'll put it all together and you'll find some helpful questions to encourage (or force!) you to think it all through.

ONLY ONE THING IS NEEDED

I said earlier that there would be no ranking. But actually, there does need to be one. There is one non-negotiable in how we spend our time, which Jesus makes clear during his stay with two friends, Martha and Mary:

> [38] As Jesus and his disciples were on their way, he came to a village where a woman named Martha opened her home to him. [39] She had a sister called Mary, who sat at the Lord's feet listening to what he said. [40] But Martha was distracted by all the preparations that had to be made. She came to him and asked, "Lord, don't you care that my sister has left me to do the work by myself? Tell her to help me!"
>
> [41] "Martha, Martha," the Lord answered, "you are worried and upset about many things, [42] but few things are needed—or indeed only one. Mary has chosen what is better, and it will not be taken away from her."
>
> (Luke 10 v 38-42)

In all of life's duties and demands, there is only one supreme necessity. Other demands upon us should be neglected in favour of the one essential activity: listening to Jesus. "Few things are needed," says Jesus. "Indeed only one." And it is Mary who has done it—she "sat at the Lord's feet listening to what he said".

The truth is that you and I could live above the "floor to obedience" as spouse, parent, employee, neighbour, friend and church member... and yet still be disobedient if we're not spending time with Jesus. Yet how easy it is, when we're really busy, to let time with Jesus be one of the first things that slips off our agenda.

That's what Martha had done. Martha is a wonderful, wholehearted believer and yet she still gets this wrong. You can easily imagine the scene. Martha is thrilled that Jesus is coming, and she is desperate to put on a feast for him. No doubt she is driven by a mixture of pride and love for Jesus; our motives too are often mixed. All her time is spent on preparing the best welcome she can for her Lord—so much so that she is driven to irritation with Mary, and accuses Jesus of not caring.

Personally, I find that these five verses skewer me. It is very easy to be engaged in plenty of good and useful activities for the Lord, but fail to spend any time actually listening to him or speaking to him, and become irritated with others for not being equally consumed with activity for him.

I need to be reminded of what Martha needed to remember: time with Jesus is more important than time spent preparing a banquet for him. It is better to be a listening disciple than a perfect hostess, or a successful businessman, or winner of "Parent of the Year" in some magazine, or a "go-to" guy at church whenever a job needs doing. We must not allow our activity—even our activity for Jesus—to distract us from time with Jesus.

There are many calls upon our time, but only one thing is needed—to sit at the feet of Jesus and listen to his word. Amid the hectic pace of this life, listening to Jesus is the one thing that will help me make sensible use of each day.

Please don't make the mistake of thinking that finding time to spend with the Lord is just one more thing you now need to squeeze into your day, another burden. The great preacher Charles Spurgeon once observed that the exhausted man never finds it a burden to rest on a chair.

After a late night, the party girl never finds it a burden to collapse into her bed. After a long day, the worn-out commuter never finds it a burden to collapse on the sofa. The fractious toddler never finds it a burden to fall asleep resting her head on her mum's lap.

It is never a burden to come and listen to Jesus. If we view it that way, we have probably forgotten who he is. He offers us "rest" as we come to him. Time with him is time that restores us, reshapes us and refreshes us. Time with Jesus reminds us of how wonderful he is; and that however full our day, and however well or badly it goes, he is all we need. He is a glorious Saviour who is worth following. He is a generous Master who is worth serving. He is a wise Teacher who is worth listening to. Time with him will strengthen us for the day ahead, help us re-order our priorities and keep the troubles of the day in perspective.

A businessman in our church puts it in blunt terms: "If I spend time with the Lord each morning, I am less anxious and make better decisions. It is a terrible use of my time to skip my time of Bible and prayer."

So, before we jump into the complexities of juggling family, work, church and leisure commitments, let's be clear that few things are strictly needed—indeed only one. We must make time to listen to the voice of Jesus. Compared with that, the rest of our time is spent on details.

7. TIME FOR WORK

The author Robert Banks tells the story of Horace Whittell, a dockworker from Gillingham, England, who hated his alarm clock. Every day for 47 years, he had been jarred awake by its shrill bell. So on the day he retired, he took it into work and flattened it under an 80-ton hydraulic press. "It was a lovely feeling," he said. I can imagine.

The Bible's view of work lines up with what most of us experience: it can be great, and it can be frustrating. Crucially for this book, it is only one arena of life. In the West today, work has become so tightly tied to our sense of worth that it is hard for us to make objective decisions about how long we should spend there.

In this chapter we're thinking about paid work. It's not the only work we do; we'll think about housework, paperwork, and other things such as DIY elsewhere. Yet for most of us, paid work is the largely immovable block in the week that we have least control over. Although the average hours worked in the UK are

43 per week and 46 in the US, one in eight of us works more than 50 hours per week. That's more work than sleep for some!

DRAWING SOME LINES

It's impossible to reach too many conclusions about time at work until we've looked at all the major arenas of life, but we can begin to put some biblical parameters in place. For some, the reality is that unless we set boundaries to our time in paid work, it will fill the whole of our lives. It's a tricky balance, but we want to make sure we live in the big area of freedom between the lines of neglect and idolatry.

Some lines are easy to put in place. One simple way of falling short is refusing to work and so being dependent upon others. Paul tells one church:

> We hear that some among you are idle and disruptive. They are not busy; they are busybodies. Such people we command and urge in the Lord Jesus Christ to settle down and earn the food they eat.
>
> (2 Thessalonians 3 v 11-12)

He's not talking about periods of unwanted unemployment, but a decision not to work and to live off the labour of others.

At the other extreme, we've already touched upon workaholism in chapter four. The word "workaholic" was coined in 1971 by Wayne Oates, who admitted in *Confessions of a Workaholic: The Facts about Work Addiction* that on one occasion his enterprising young son was so desperate to see him that he made an appointment at his dad's clinic through his receptionist. It was the only way the child felt that he could get to see his dad!

Most of us are not at either of these extremes though—so how much time should we spend working if we're going to be faithful? Let's turn to another of Paul's letters, written to the church in Ephesus:

> ⁵ Slaves, obey your earthly masters with respect and fear, and with sincerity of heart, just as you would obey Christ. ⁶ Obey them not only to win their favour when their eye is on you, but as slaves of Christ, doing the will of God from your heart. ⁷ Serve wholeheartedly, as if you were serving the Lord, not people, ⁸ because you know that the Lord will reward each one for whatever good they do, whether they are slave or free.
>
> ⁹ And masters, treat your slaves in the same way. Do not threaten them, since you know that he who is both their Master and yours is in heaven, and there is no favouritism with him. (Ephesians 6 v 5-9)

The key line here is: "Serve wholeheartedly, as if you were serving the Lord, not people". The message is: don't be an "eye-pleaser", don't be a "people-pleaser", but instead be a "Lord-pleaser". Paul is basically introducing us to three different workers, with very different motivations for working.

1. "EYE-PLEASING"

The "eye-pleaser" is the employee who only works when the boss is watching. This is falling below the floor of obedience into neglect. They are quite happy to spend their day bidding on eBay, poking on Facebook and tweeting on Twitter until the boss or client comes. All of a sudden, they double the speed at which they're painting walls or tapping away at their keyboards. That is merely eye-pleasing—and we know it's wrong.

One modern manifestation of this can be "working from home". In the UK, over half of employers now offer "teleworking" for some or part of the working week. Of course, it's very easy for "working from home" to turn into childcare for their kids or shopping online, and then sending one email every half hour to make it look as if they are busy.

Another dangerous time for eye-pleasing is if we are approaching retirement. When I was a schoolteacher, it made me sad to observe the occasional colleague in their late fifties going through the motions. It was laziness with a hint of action when the boss was nearby. The upshot was that they were miserable, their classes were miserable and their results were miserable. That's lose-lose-lose!

2. "PEOPLE-PLEASING"

For many, though, and especially in demanding jobs, the greater issue is "people-pleasing". This worker works very hard, all the time, because they want to impress the boss. This way lies preferment, promotion, and pay rises. But Paul does not say that your boss is your Lord. Rather, the Christian works as if for the Lord. We cannot say: "I work hard, and God loves that". God cares about our heart's motives as well as our hands' work. The Lord only loves hard work if it's for him, not if our motive for hard work is self-gain or people-pleasing. Ultimately, your employer is not Lord of your time. Jesus is.

One extreme example is that of Moritz Erhaldt. A 21-year-old intern, he made the news in 2013 when he died after working for 72 hours straight, without any sleep. He was undertaking a seven-week internship at Bank of America in London. Apparently, he had pulled a number of all-nighters in an attempt to impress his boss. It was a fatal mistake. He worked hard but clearly not in a way that was healthy and not in a manner that honoured the Lord. This was tragic—and yet is an (extreme) example of a work machismo that can exist in some people's minds.

For most, people-pleasing isn't literally a killer; but it does kill relationships, including our one with God. If you're driven by your people-pleasing, you will cut corners in your obedience to Jesus.

3. "LORD-PLEASING"

This is where we want to be. Serving the Lord will mean wholeheartedly serving your boss, yet not allowing them to be Lord of your time. It must also mean fulfilling other God-given responsibilities. It's good to be ambitious—but we must be clear who we are ambitious to please. It's good to work hard to have a successful career, but not at the expense of other aspects of godly living. Long hours cannot be justified if:

1. other God-given obligations are forsaken.
2. long hours are pursued for idolatrous reasons.

We'll have to wait until we've considered the other arenas of life before we see as individuals how work may be causing us to fall below the floor to obedience in other parts of life. But if, as you read the next few chapters, you realise that your job consistently forces you elsewhere below the "floor to obedience" and into neglect, then something needs to change.

For now, let's start to consider the second issue: how can we know if we're working idolatrously? Let's briefly consider four factors that can often rear their heads and cause us to overwork. They can be remembered by the slightly cringe-worthy letters M.E.G.A. We'll not be guilty of all of them (I hope!) but they can help us understand the pressures upon us.

MEANING

A growing trend this century has been the encouragement to do a job that you love. It sounds good but can encourage the sense that work defines who I am. Here's the late Steve Jobs, the CEO of Apple, giving a graduation speech to students from Stanford University in 2005:

You've got to find what you love. And that is as true for your work as it is for your lovers. Your work is going to fill a large part of your life, and the only way to be truly satisfied is to do what you believe is great work. And the only way to do great work is to love what you do.

Now, that sounds great for a CEO of a cool company, or indeed a graduate from a top university, but how does that apply to sweat-shop workers doing an 80-hour week and sleeping six to a room? How does it work if you leave school at sixteen with barely an education? "Do a job that you love" is unrealistic for most people. Yet it creates a pressure to discover "the *perfect* job", to put in hours at work that can get you there, and to consider life a failure until you do.

If we swallow the "do what you love" view of work, and yet find ourselves doing a boring task or in a dull job, then we have a ready-made excuse to be lazy—to become an eye-pleaser. It's so easy to think: *If I'm not doing work I love, then it's not work I should be doing—so maybe I won't bother...*

And if and when we do land the dream job, we will only be disappointed. This view of work expects too much, because no job can offer true satisfaction. Remember Helen Mirren in chapter two? She has achieved everything in her chosen line of work—but she has not found satisfaction along the way. Not many workplaces look like the set of *Glee*, with staff spontaneously bursting into song in order to sing of the joy they find in their work. There are good days and bad days. Work will never provide the fulfilment we desire.

Ironically, the more you do love your work—the more meaning you derive from it—the more danger there is of idolatry in this way. The closer we get to what we're told to chase, the more dangerous it becomes. This can be a particular danger to those in "caring" professions. Nurses, social workers, relief workers or pastors can feel that there is a greater inherent nobility to their work. They can directly see the good it does, and so it is easy to justify overwork. It's possible for idolatry to grow under a label called "nobility".

ENVY

The Teacher in Ecclesiastes writes:

> And I saw that all toil and all achievement spring from one person's envy of another. This too is meaningless, a chasing after the wind.
> Fools fold their hands and ruin themselves.
> Better one handful with tranquillity
>> than two handfuls with toil and chasing after the wind.
>
> (4 v 4-6)

Often, what drives us is envious comparison with others. Of course, envy does sometimes drive us to achieve success. But it is not a success that satisfies. However much you grab—status, pay, power—there will always be someone with bigger hands.

According to a recent book by Oxford University professor Danny Dorling, half of those in the top 1% of earners in the UK are miserable with envy. To enter this group in the UK, you need to earn £160,000 per year. Most of those tend to be in the global banking industry, and so gravitate to only socialising with a narrow mix of people. This creates incredible competition and envy. Often those in the lower half of the top 1% of earners don't feel rich. They envy the wealth of those in the top 0.5% and so work ever harder to break into that group. They have what you probably think would be more than enough (and maybe are working really hard to get towards). They are earning between £160,000 to £330,000 and don't feel rich. They chase more. They chase the wind. And millions more do the same, lower down the pay scale.

GREED

Again, let's listen to the Teacher:

> I saw something meaningless under the sun:
> there was a man all alone;
>> he had neither son nor brother.
> There was no end to his toil,
>> yet his eyes were not content with his wealth.
> "For whom am I toiling," he asked,
>> "and why am I depriving myself of enjoyment?"
> This too is meaningless—a miserable business!
>
> (Ecclesiastes 4 v 7-8)

What a tragic picture of a man toiling away for wealth, yet never being content. Of course, working for wealth sounds too crass for a Christian. It is more likely to manifest as: *I'm working to pay the rent or mortgage; I'm working to afford a great holiday; I'm working for the new kitchen; I'm working to provide for the children's education.* Very few people self-identify as being driven by greed.

But the greedy person often ends up as "a man [or woman]

all alone". The truly tragic thing about this man is that he has no one to share his wealth with. Maybe his wife has left him because of his overwork and because he was clearly more excited by his career than by her. Maybe he never makes the time to phone old friends or meet up with them, because investing in friendship never makes it near the top of the to-do list. The temptation to take on an extra shift this week or to take on a new project is a powerful one. The extra money would be really useful. Yet we can kill off our relationships in this way.

ANXIETY

One poll undertaken by a hotel chain discovered that eight out of ten seasoned travellers take a work mobile phone on holiday with them. Four out of ten take their work laptop.

Now, I can see why that might be the case in the middle of a crisis. I can see why a president or prime minister needs to be in contact with the office. Yet for most of us, to regularly have that level of attachment to the office is crazy. Why do we do it? I think it's because of fear. Fear of what our life actually consists of without work. Fear of what might go wrong without us being there to sort it out; and perhaps under that, fear that we're actually not that important and our company can function perfectly well without us for a while.

We do need to be honest about work pressure. There were times in the last recession when plenty of people feared for their jobs and their firms. It was a real concern, not just a felt one. But remember, we have a choice: do we go to work anxious, or trusting? Often that choice has a practical edge: do I check my work emails daily on holiday, or do I not?

Moritz Erhaldt was driven to his death at Bank of America by *anxiety*. In his online profile he wrote that he came from a family "that expected me, in whatever respect, to excel in my life. By implication, I feel somewhat pressurised." His was not a fear of letting down his boss. He was working far harder than his boss expected. It was a fear of letting down his family which drove him to be anxious in his work.

However, for some of us that fear has simply become habit. We check office emails not because we're a president handling the threat of invasion, but because we've programmed ourselves to do it.

When we're battling one or more of these M.E.G.A. factors, we need to return to the truths in the first part of this book, especially chapters 3 – 5. We need to know that Christ is the source of rest. We go to work trusting in him, not ourselves. We need to long to promote Christ and be part of his eternal kingdom-building, not to win promotion for ourselves as we build our own, tiny, temporary empire. This world is fleeting and our real desire is to achieve something that lasts into eternity.

WORKING WITH FREEDOM

So far, then, our parameters are shaping up like this:

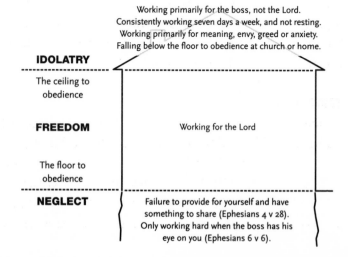

Working primarily for the boss, not the Lord.
Consistently working seven days a week, and not resting.
Working primarily for meaning, envy, greed or anxiety.
Falling below the floor to obedience at church or home.

IDOLATRY

The ceiling to obedience

FREEDOM

Working for the Lord

The floor to obedience

NEGLECT

Failure to provide for yourself and have something to share (Ephesians 4 v 28). Only working hard when the boss has his eye on you (Ephesians 6 v 6).

That still leaves a huge grey area of "freedom" to explore—an area where we're free to decide what is wise for us when it comes to work. We need to look at other arenas of life to help guide us here, but let me begin to make some suggestions. We'll need to return to these in chapter 11, but, for now, what might guide your choices between the floor and the ceiling?

SHARING THE GOSPEL?

Those of us in secular employment are not paid to share the gospel with our colleagues; we're paid to serve our employer. Yet it would be very odd if Christians did not seek to make the most use of every opportunity to tell others about Jesus.

However, sometimes we're simply in "work-mode" and don't notice the opportunity. It passes us by and afterwards we think, "if only". Other times we know that we could explain the gospel to a colleague—maybe even read the Bible with them one to one—but the pay-off will be staying later in the office and seeing less of family and friends. Surely that's the right thing sometimes. As one family man put it to me recently: "Opportunities to share the gospel at work are scarce. Work is never scarce; there is always more that can be done. I need to grab hold of the scarce opportunities when they come." There's realism there! It's daft to pass up the rare opportunity of sharing the gospel, when it comes.

GROWING A MINISTRY?

Another way of using your freedom is to invest in a gospel ministry. One university lecturer at our church knows that he could accelerate his career and his salary if he jumped institutions. Loyalty is not rewarded in his profession—you have to jump around to progress rapidly. However, he has stayed working at the same university for the whole of his career. Why take the hit? Because he has a really useful ministry among the students at the university. It would take time to rebuild that elsewhere and he could end up being less useful to the kingdom. He has stayed and accepted slower promotion and a lower wage because he can serve the Lord really effectively by staying.

That is not a particularly common decision for people to take. No one is obliged to copy him, but he's certainly asking the right question: *How can I most usefully serve the Lord?* I predict that, in eternity, he'll be delighted with the decision he took.

PLANNING FOR THE FUTURE?

Some people take the choice to use all their freedom now to work, with the hope that it allows them greater freedom later. For example, there's the secretary who does an evening class for a year to improve IT skills to get a more highly paying job, or the worker who busts a gut to achieve a promotion that enables him to have more control over the hours he works. I know of some who have worked crazy hours in a demanding company before having a family, with the plan that when children come along, their resumé will look good and they can obtain part-time work more easily.

All of those can be fine. My one caution would be that it's easy to get used to operating in a certain way and to put up with the "all consuming job" longer than you had planned. If you're investing heavily in work for a fixed time, get someone to hold you accountable on when that time's going to end.

INVESTING IN YOUR FAMILY?

A recent survey on work-life balance from Warwick University was very interesting on this point. 67% of British workers said that they wanted to spend more time with their family. In the US the figure was 85%.

And yet, for many people, there is a choice! Not an easy one—not a common one to take. Yet there is a choice, and it is to earn less and see your family more. Perhaps it would involve having a less interesting job, or downsizing your house. It's not a choice that has only one correct decision. But recognise that often there *is* a choice. Sometimes we won't consider it or can't even see it.

The Lord grants us great freedom in our use of time. Many of us have freedom about when and where to work. But some of us probably need to recognise that unless we set boundaries to our work, it will enforce boundaries upon us. And those boundaries will force us beneath the floor of obedience in some other area of our life. Work is good, and often fun. But it is not your god, and will never fulfil you.

8. TIME FOR FAMILY

Hook is not a classic film (in my humble opinion); nor is it a great tear-jerker. So I think my son was surprised, as we watched it together one wet Saturday afternoon, to see me a little moist-eyed at the end.

What got to me was the character played by the late, great Robin Williams: Peter Banning. Peter is a successful corporate lawyer. His work is all demanding, and so his relationship with his wife and kids is in trouble as he repeatedly breaks his promises of time with them. Early on, we see him exiting his daughter's school production in order to take a phone call. He sends someone from work to record his son's baseball game, which he had promised not to miss. We see him shouting at his kids to be quiet while making an important call on his mobile phone.

Events take a strange turn when Peter's children are stolen by Captain Hook and taken to Neverland. Peter pursues them and seeks to rescue them, only to find that they don't want to return with him. They are fed up with his long absences and broken promises. Eventually, Peter rediscovers the joy of being a father, and everyone is reconciled in a happily-ever-after, "haven't we all learned to be better people" sort of way.

Here's why I was a little moist-eyed—because for me, there is just enough resemblance to my own behaviour in Peter's to make me squirm, and to make me sad.

Of course, not all parents make the "Peter-Banning-mistake". But there is an equal and opposite error. It's possible for our lives to revolve around our families to the detriment of other commitments and responsibilities. Many parents are familiar with being a taxi service to various clubs and activities, but increasingly people wonder about the healthiness of a child-centred world. A newspaper columnist commented recently that their eight-year-old daughter was doing a project at school titled: "All about me". It was the second time in her school career that she had done a project about herself. It can't be healthy having kids grow up thinking that life is all about them, nor for parents to indulge or even encourage this sentiment.

We're going to see what God has to say about our relationships with spouses, children and parents. Most of us will have one of those three commitments; many will have more than one. It may be that you only want to consider the sections that apply to you. But before we jump in, let me say that what you won't find here are rules, but principles; and those principles will apply differently to different families in varying circumstances. The demands of a family with three pre-school children and elderly parents are very different from that of a family whose children have left the nest.

LOVING SPOUSES

> Husbands, love your wives, just as Christ loved the
> church and gave himself up for her to make her holy,
> cleansing her by the washing with water through the
> word. (Ephesians 5 v 25-26)

The Bible sets a high bar for husbands—love your wife as Jesus loves his people. A husband is to sacrifice for his wife—not primarily to make her comfortable, but for her spiritual good.

How does that apply to time? A neglected spouse will be a resentful one, frustrated and unlikely to grow in godliness. You've dropped below the floor of obedience into neglect if your spouse is regularly irritated at how little time you get together, and yet you never take any steps to talk it through or make changes.

It is impossible to prescribe here. One wife may have a husband who works 80 hours a week, yet she is content. Another may have a husband who works 40 hours and yet is grumpy that he's never around. The crucial thing is that you agree your work patterns with your spouse. You both have to have signed up to the job and its commitments. The same goes for commitments to church (once we're above the floor of obedience), hobbies, and so on.

I can think of one family I know where the husband is in a demanding job and can sometimes take work calls when with the family. One year, when on holiday overseas, he couldn't find his phone, which he needed to make a call back to the office. Eventually he asked his wife: "Do you know where my phone is?" Her reply? "Yep, it's sitting in the padded envelope I placed it in before posting it back to your office in the UK. I think it's time to enjoy our holiday."

At this point I believe they had a "frank and open discussion..." But there is a lesson to be learned. You've got to agree your use of time with your spouse.

That same passage has a word for wives, too:

Wives, submit yourselves to your own husbands as you do to the Lord. (Ephesians 5 v 22)

Much of what I've just said about husbands is true, in time terms, of wives too. Yet a Christian wife is, in a way that goes against the culture, called to allow her husband to lead their marriage, as he seeks to sacrifice himself for his wife's good. There are plenty of marriages where the wife earns more than the husband and is committed to working longer hours. Sometimes that can create an awkward dynamic as she spends more time at work than him and appears to be much more of a leader than him. It doesn't need to cause tension but often it can do. You need to talk about this and reach a place where you're both happy.

Years ago, before we had any children, we reached a point in marriage where my wife Ceri and I were not spending enough time together. Between my six days a week in ministry and her long five days a week in work we found little time for fun. Saturday was the only joint day off and we had chores to do such as shopping, DIY and bill paying. We decided that the easiest way to create some time was for Ceri to drop to four days a week. We could afford to do it, with some adjustments— and it created the slack we needed to rediscover that we still loved each other!

Of course, it's not merely work that can cause us to neglect time with our spouses. Sometimes it's selfish entertainment. I talk to plenty of couples where there is frustration that "she spends loads of time on Facebook" or "he wastes time on computer games". The upshot is that chores don't get done, or there's no time given to actually talking to one another. Sometimes loving your wife and respecting your husband is as simple as turning off the TV or computer that you're watching on your own, and going to bed at the same time as them.

One last thing. It's quite easy to neglect your spouse day by day without anything seeming to be wrong. If you neglect your kids, they're faster to play up or cry out. If you neglect your work, then someone will let you know. However, it's possible to neglect your spouse for quite some time before you really notice that your marriage has deteriorated. Perhaps you need to stop reading and ask your spouse: "How are we doing? How can I love you better?"

NOURISHING CHILDREN

> Fathers, do not exasperate your children; instead, bring
> them up in the training and instruction of the Lord.
>
> (Ephesians 6 v 4)

TOO LITTLE

There are many things that can exasperate children: parents being overly harsh or inconsistent in applying rules and discipline. But near the top of the list is the "Peter-Banning-mistake"—serial absenteeism or, more acutely, breaking promises of spending time with your children. To do this more than very rarely is to fall below the line of obedience.

And it's possible to be absent while being present. It's easy to fool ourselves and think we're with our families when our minds are elsewhere.

Mike often takes the kids to the park on a Saturday morning while his wife has some down time. He commented to me recently that he had allowed this to become a check-box exercise. "Good dad playing with his kids?" Check. But the problem was that although he was physically present, he was mentally absent. Although he was with his family, he was playing with his phone and daydreaming about work. How exasperating—and saddening—it must be for a toddler to want to share a moment of joy on the swings with their parent, only to find their parent consulting that little black box again.

Beyond that, few things are as exasperating in life as not being understood. Part of parenting is to understand the world our children inhabit—and that takes time. What are the pressures upon them? What is cool and what is not? Are they noble things or ungodly? We'll never do this perfectly (has there ever been a teenager who says their parents understand them perfectly?!), but a failure to take time to engage with our kids in their world can easily lead them to become exasperated. Wise parents make meeting around the table for meals a central activity in family life.

By contrast, Paul tells parents, or fathers in particular, to "bring up"—or more literally, "nourish"—their children in the training and instruction of the Lord. It's the same word that Paul uses of his own ministry elsewhere (1 Thessalonians 2 v 7). Fathers are to take a lead in ensuring that children are modelled Christian living and taught biblical truth. Mothers will inevitably be involved in this work—and sometimes for some reason there is no father around—but fathers should not abdicate their own role. They need to be seen by their children to take a lead.

In my observations, few Christian families deliberately avoid the training and instruction of the Lord, yet it can get squeezed out. I had a very honest conversation with a dad recently. He commented that for most of the week he is a leader in the office. People look to him to set the agenda and order priorities and he rarely lets them down. Yet, he observed, by the time the weekend comes:

I'm utterly exhausted and I'm nervous that although we're at church every week, what I'm modelling to my children is: "Work is where the action is; church is the place you go when you're walloped." Something needs to change.

Yes, it does. I think this father had got a lot further than many parents, though, who haven't even noticed, or don't care enough to be "nervous". A failure to rightly nourish children in the Lord is falling below the floor of obedience.

You may be reading this section and hoping I'll deal with the question: *What about working mothers? Is that a good use of time?* Can I plead for some generosity and understanding on this topic? It shocks me how much heat this generates. This area seems to make many mums feel guilty—some for going out to work and "neglecting" their kids; others for not earning money for their family.

Perhaps we need to accept some reality, and then recognise some freedom. The reality is that none of us can have it all. For years, though, women were told that they could "have it all"—full-time jobs, loving marriages and happy kids. Yet in the last few years, a new honesty has emerged. Sheryl Sandberg of Facebook is one of the most high-profile women in the business world today, and actively encourages women to rise to the top of business. Yet she recently observed:

No one can have it all. That language is the worst thing that's happened to the women's movement.

From a mother at the top of the business world, that's a helpful dose of honesty.

Another reality is that for some families, two incomes are a financial necessity. If Family X are going to be able to stay in an area and remain committed to their church, they need two incomes to pay the bills. You could tell them to move to a cheaper city or a cheaper part of town, but often that's unrealistic given other family or church commitments. Perhaps they could tweak their lifestyles somewhat, but overall, let's cut them some slack.

Of course, for other families, earning two incomes is not out of necessity, but it does allow financial improvement. A mum might feel that at a certain stage of her kid's lives, she could combine earning with school pick ups, in a way which benefits the whole family or in a way which enables them to give generously to Christian ministry. Now this could simply be raw greed... or it could be a godly decision to earn money that benefits the family and the kingdom. We need to challenge our own motives in our decisions here, and be willing to have friends challenge our thinking. But equally, please do not think the worst of other families when you don't understand their situation.

Still other families have taken the decision that it is better to have both mum and dad working steadily than have dad working crazy hours to generate all of the income they need. That way, both get to spend some good time with the kids and neither gets too stressed out by work. I know of some families where both mum and dad work part-time and share childcare. I can think of other families where the dad has taken a pay cut in order to secure an accompanying "hours cut", and then the salary difference is made up by the wife working part-time.

My point is that there are some realities to face up to; and then there is a lot of freedom. The Bible neither says mothers must not work, nor that they should. What it does say is that your decisions should not force you below the line of obedience in this area or another.

TOO MUCH

Although it's easy to fall into neglect in parenting, it's also easy to swing over into obsessing and idolatry.

I like the writer and presenter Giles Coren. He's funny and provocative. He wrote an article a few months ago on being a dad and described it in stark terms:

Nothing I do matters apart from being a father. It's not that being a father matters more, it is that nothing else matters at all ... I devote every available second to being a father. I do not work after 5pm or at the weekend, ever. And never will ... Nor even does being a husband matter. My wife could easily find another one.

I imagine he was exaggerating for the sake of a newspaper article; but actually, I think he reflects one fairly common, sometimes subconscious, attitude: it's all about the family. The kids come first. And that is to set up our children as an idol.

The ironic truth is that idolising a child is not good for the child. In general, turning your kid into an idol leads to one of three negative outcomes:

1. You crush them with your expectations of achieving great things or succeeding where you failed.
2. You let the world crush them. You indulge them, you let them get their way, and you ensure they're ill equipped to deal with the real world, where they don't win all the time.
3. You are crushed when they take decisions that are different to yours or they don't become the people you

had expected. They declare at some point or other: "I *hate* you"; they leave home and don't call as much as you would hope. And since your whole life was wrapped up in them, you unravel.

In simple terms, idolatry of our kids is sin! Jesus declares what our priorities must look like:

> Anyone who loves their father or mother more than me is not worthy of me; anyone who loves their son or daughter more than me is not worthy of me.
>
> (Matthew 10 v 37)

And not only does worshipping our children mean we don't worship Jesus as we should, but it also impacts on the rest of our life. Taken at face value, Giles Coren's willingness to have his life revolve around his daughter means he is willing to neglect responsibilities at work and to his spouse. I'm sure he's not the only one.

For Christian families, an idolatrous obsession with children is sometimes seen in regularly prioritising sports clubs or activities over church. It's deeply frustrating that so many sports teams now take place on a Sunday, as secular society tries to replace church community with "touchline community". Yet it would seem that regularly skipping church to take the kids to football or cricket has gone beyond what's required and drifted into an idolatrous pursuit of time with/ for the kids. Your children need Jesus more than they need a professional sports contract. In fact, they need Jesus more than they need to be popular, happy, or thrilled that you are their parents. Similarly, an obsession with tutoring children, so that far more time goes on verbal reasoning or bassoon lessons than on learning of Jesus, is an indicator that loving care may have crossed the line into idolatry.

And it's very easy to bounce back and forth between "too little" and "too much". If parents begin to become aware that they have been overworking and perhaps neglecting the kids, it can very easily cause an over-compensation, so that the same parents then lavish time upon their children to the neglect of all else.

TOO GUILTY?

Let me add a caution. I think it's easier to make people feel guilty over their parenting than almost anything else. To make a mess of a job is depressing, but those of us who are parents tend to fear making a mess of parenthood far more. To some people, I need to say: *Stop it. Stop feeling guilty. If you're avoiding exasperating your children and are nourishing them in the training and instruction of the Lord, then you are doing a good job, you are pleasing God, and you need to stop feeling guilty.*

Personally, I know that my own feelings of guilt in parenting rise up for one of three reasons:

1. I am guilty! I'm exasperating my family by neglecting them. Answer? I need to stop feeling bad and do something about my mistakes. I need to repent, apologise and rearrange my schedule.
2. My feeble pride means I want to be known as a good dad and I want my son to tell me I'm a great dad. Answer? I need to repent of my ego, and instead of over-analysing every day off with the family to see how well I did, I should fix my eyes upon Jesus.
3. I legalistically panic that the salvation of my children depends upon me alone and therefore am driven by fear of them rejecting Jesus. Answer? I need to repent of my legalism, rest in Jesus and then do a faithful job of parenting.

You do know that you don't have to go to every school play or concert, don't you? It's a lovely thing to be able to do. Your kids may feel disappointed if you never go and so it may be a wise decision to plan to attend sometimes. Yet missing a few does not make you a bad parent.

I'm always impressed with parents who have multiple kids and manage to regularly schedule in one-to-one time with each child—a hot chocolate here, a shopping trip there, a camping night thrown in. That sounds great. It may well be wise, especially as children enter teenage years and communication can become harder. Yet, none of these things are required biblically. If you don't do them, that's okay.

Maybe you need to repent, as I so often do. But remember that Jesus offers rest. He gives forgiveness. He can fix any mess you've caused and make up for any mistakes you've made. So repent, and don't feel guilty. Instead, get on with not exasperating, actively nourishing, and working out how to spend your time wisely to avoid the first and pursue the second.

Overall, the Bible does not state how much time you should spend with your family. It simply says, invest enough time so that your spouse knows that they're loved, that your children are not exasperated and that you are nourishing them in the faith. Different spouses and different children will require varying amounts of time to achieve these things. If we don't reach agreement on use of time with our families, then we're likely to store up resentment.

HONOURING PARENTS

"Honour your father and mother"—which is the first commandment with a promise. (Ephesians 6 v 2)

What does it mean to honour your parents? That varies between cultures and families. For example, I read that the Chinese government passed an "Elderly Rights Law" in 2013. The law requires that after parents reach the age of 60, grown-up children are legally obliged to visit them "frequently". Failure to do so and provide for their "daily and spiritual needs" could land you in prison!

Of course, there's a little part of all of us that would love there to be a straightforward rule that we could keep: "Phone your parents twice a week until the age of 30, when it can be reduced to one phone call or Skype conversation at the weekend." "Go to their house for Christmas every other year, or every third year if you have children."

Of course it doesn't work that way. As with every other area we've looked at, there are some seasons when parents will need far more of our time than at others. My father is currently undergoing several rounds of chemotherapy. Naturally, we're going to visit him and my mother more frequently than we used to. They need encouragement and we're also conscious that we don't know how much more time he may have left. That may mean less overtime at work, or less time with Ceri, my wife. A few years ago it was completely different. Mum and Dad would come to us and help out with childcare; they would "add time" to our lives.

Of course, parents are also able to apply unreasonable de-mands upon their adult children. I can think of a few individu-als who have been shocked after the wedding day to discover that their new in-laws would love to see them every weekend.

Honouring parents does not mean a blank time-cheque. If doing all they ask (or command) will push you below the floor of obedience in other parts of our lives, then a difficult conversation needs to be had—gently, lovingly, but firmly.

FREEDOM IN FAMILY TIME

Let's put it all together in our "house" image over the page. We've seen the floor to obedience and the ceiling of obedience for both work and home now. And it may be that as you think about these two areas you're already feeling squeezed, time-wise. But please don't panic—we're only going to add two more!

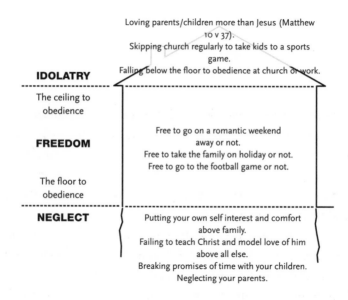

IDOLATRY

Loving parents/children more than Jesus (Matthew 10 v 37).
Skipping church regularly to take kids to a sports game.
Falling below the floor to obedience at church or work.

The ceiling to obedience

FREEDOM

Free to go on a romantic weekend away or not.
Free to take the family on holiday or not.
Free to go to the football game or not.

The floor to obedience

NEGLECT

Putting your own self interest and comfort above family.
Failing to teach Christ and model love of him above all else.
Breaking promises of time with your children.
Neglecting your parents.

9. TIME FOR CHURCH

It's very easy to get away with being half-hearted about church.

If you don't put in the hours at work, your boss will soon let you know. If you don't spend time with your immediate family, your kids will let you know with their behaviour if not their words. If you neglect your spouse or parents, they'll endure it for a time, but a reckoning will come.

By contrast, it's easier to ignore church—to turn up a bit less often, and to do a bit less while we're there—without being badgered by anyone. When time gets squeezed, it's hard to reduce hours at work or ignore the family, so church is the arena where time can get culled. Yet, what if God knows best, and when he tells us to meet regularly and to serve intentionally, it is for our good and, in many ways, reviving?

Often the time we feel we "gain" on a Sunday does us little good. A recent survey revealed that the "Sunday blues" (due to the impending return to work) begin, on average, at 4:13pm on a Sunday. This probably isn't helped by the fact that 75% of UK residents don't bother leaving the house on a Sunday at all!

By contrast, Christians have traditionally viewed Sunday as the first day of the week, one that equips them for the other six. It makes quite a difference to view things that way rather than viewing Monday as the first day of a five-day week, with two days at the end to collapse and recover. Regardless of your views on Sunday as a "Sabbath", the New Testament certainly sees Sunday as the first day of the week (for instance, Matthew 28 v 1). In an earlier generation, our Christian forefathers viewed Sunday as "the marketplace of the soul"—the primary time to gather spiritually what we need to serve Jesus in the remainder of the week. In the Christian life, church isn't an optional extra; it's an absolute essential.

So, what is the floor and ceiling to faithful use of our time at church?

MEETING TOGETHER

> And let us consider how we may spur one another on towards love and good deeds, not giving up meeting together, as some are in the habit of doing, but encouraging one another—and all the more as you see the Day approaching. (Hebrews 10 v 24-25)

The first sentence of this passage gets smoothed out in translation. The literal meaning is more like: "Let us consider one another to spur one another." That's a lot of thinking about other people! The writer used the same verb in 3 v 1, where he tells us to "consider Jesus" (ESV). Regular thinking about Jesus is central to Christian living; but we're called to think regularly about others at church, too, in order to spur them on.

Normal Christian living will involve praying for and thinking about the best way to encourage fellow believers, even before we get together. Maybe it's time to take the headphones off and daydream about people a little more as we wander down the road.

At the most simple level, these verses are clear that neglecting to meet together falls below the floor of obedience for the Christian. I'm sure we know that, yet some of us need to be more honestly realistic about this. I meet lots of people who call themselves "regulars" at church; but their definition of regular is about one week in three. That's not what the writer to the Hebrews means. If we're committed to spurring one another on—if we regularly think through how we might do that—then we'll need to see each other very regularly.

There are multiple reasons why people can get into the habit of missing church. We'll return later to the pressures of family and work competing with church. Yet sometimes it's things as simple as "wanting to finish off a bit of DIY" or: "I can get a cheaper ticket if I travel on a Sunday". I'm also surprised when Christians skip church because family members are visiting and "they won't like it". The Sunday meeting is not all day, and there is of course the chance that they might find it interesting—and they'll certainly continue to see church as unimportant and irrelevant if you feel happy to skip it!

For some people, especially those in their twenties, it's often travel that keeps them from regular commitment at church. I watch people at this age drive miles up and down the country, catching up with friends from school or university and becoming exhausted by their touring. Sometimes it's just travelling to other cities for a weekend to take in the sights. There's no law against such things! But some people will always make it back for church on a Sunday night, even though it means curtailing their time away slightly, while others will never bother.

So it's not a case of what's possible, but what your priorities are. Many of us have moved around a fair bit in our lives. We need to accept that we simply can't keep up with everyone, and that we do need to live where we are. One mum at our church, whose husband's job has involved them moving regularly, said to me recently: "When you've travelled as much as we have, you realise that you have to live where you are; and even if you only expect to be there for a year, live as though you'll be there for the rest of your life. Otherwise you're always pining for somewhere else." We need to invest time relationally with those around us. You have to live where you are.

We need to see one another to encourage one another. Going away for the weekend and then catching up on the sermon online does not count—who have you encouraged? Being "connected" on social media doesn't cut it either; social media can be fun and an enjoyable thing, but it is not fellowship, because it isn't real. All of us tend to put up the best pictures of ourselves and post an edited appraisal of our lives. Very few people admit to what's really going on or post online: "I was really selfish today in the way I treated my colleagues and my family". We can easily be deceived in that sort of Christian life. It's why earlier in his letter, the writer to the Hebrews warns: "Encourage one another daily, as long as it is called "Today", so that none of you may be hardened by sin's deceitfulness" (3 v 13). When we get together, people who know us can interrupt, disagree, tell us we're being daft, ask the questions we'd rather not be asked, and look us in the eye as we answer. We need to meet, not just connect.

This need for encouragement is a dominant theme of Hebrews. Encouragement is an interesting word. It can have the sense of a gentle word, such as a parent telling a child softly: "Keep going, you can do long division if you try"; or it can have a more forceful sense, such as a football coach screaming on the sidelines: "What *are* you doing?"

So to live above the floor of obedience when it comes to church, you need to meet regularly with Christians, and daydream about how to encourage them to live for Christ. In fact, simply turning up is itself an encouragement and exhortation to others, particularly if it's been a little hard to make it. Being there when it means cutting short a trip away, or when you're feeling unwell (on the basis that if you're well enough to go to work on a Monday feeling that way, you're well enough to go to church on a Sunday) says to others that you really care about them; and might prompt them to consider their own use of time and attitude to church. If you know that you can't make it, sending a text or email says to others: "I care for you and I think about how to spur you on. I'm sorry I can't make it tonight. Please pray X for me." By contrast, simply no-showing without letting anyone know might be heard as: "I'm neglecting you and haven't even considered you".

MORE THAN SUNDAYS

There's more, though—with its repeated emphasis upon "today", Hebrews reveals a view of church family that is more than just gathering in the same room once a week. It's a delight to be part of a church where people help out with childcare, visit in hospital, or write notes of biblical encouragement—in other words, share their lives. It's far easier to positively encourage and gently challenge someone's walk with Jesus when you are walking through life with them. Don't wait for your church leadership to create good church fellowship; don't think it requires a programme or committee. Take the initiative yourself by sharing your life with others.

Our church is in central London, and I've noticed that, in

our city at least, everyone talks about their desire for great friendship, yet not everyone is willing to pay the cost. Everyone seems to desire a depth of intimacy, yet not everyone is willing to accept accountability. Everyone gets fed up if people let them down, yet not everyone is willing to be committed. Christians are to be different—we are to enjoy the benefits of real friendships because we are willing to bear the costs; we are to be ready to invest in encouraging one another and serving one another.

Of course, it's impossible to suggest a general rule on how much time serving the church family is necessary to be obedient. The Bible says: "Don't neglect". We have to work out for ourselves what "neglect" looks like when it comes to our circumstances and our church. But here's one idea: I have a pastor friend who suggests that no one misses church more than six times a year for holidays. It's not a rule, but it is worth asking why we would view missing lots of time with the church family as fine when we would only take a (maximum) of six weeks holiday from work. Why is that? What does it reveal about what I think is important? Have we got that right?

Here's another idea: a middle-aged guy at our church has suggested that the monthly prayer meeting is a good litmus test for him with regard to work. He reckoned that for many busy workers a commitment such as a prayer meeting could fall into one of three boxes:

1. Tonight there's a crisis at work and no one is leaving the building (incredibly rare).
2. I can go to the prayer meeting but will make myself unpopular with my colleagues if I do (often true).
3. I am out of the habit of going to the prayer meeting because I stay and work by default (easy to slip into).

He was honest enough to admit that he had taken up all three positions at different points, but was slowly learning to examine his heart. He is also willing to be challenged by others if he isn't around. That's wisdom.

Imposing rules upon others is unlikely to be helpful; yet having some kind of litmus test for yourself can be, particularly if you ask a friend at church to encourage you by holding you accountable.

UNSUSTAINABLE CHURCH?

Let's move from the floor to the ceiling—what might be an idolatrous use of time in regard to church? Yes, it is possible to make an idol out of your church! Perhaps the most common issue is to view yourself as indispensable, in a particular ministry, area of service or pastoral issue where we think: "No one can do this except me". Often that's pride speaking, or a failure to trust God to provide.

Another way to turn church into an idol is "justification by activity". How do you know God loves you and approves of you? Is it because you are resting in Jesus and the relationship you enjoy with your Father through him; or is it because you are on ten different rotas at church, or you lead a midweek Bible-study group, or you take at least one meal round to someone else each week, or... you're the pastor? Do you serve because you know God sees and is pleased; or because you hope that others will notice, and be impressed?

The difficulty is that sometimes it's only after the event that these things become obvious. A friend called Pete is a member of a church where there are a high number of young professionals from overseas who often stay for two or three years. Pete has observed that these are often extremely eager people, who are at church meetings or with the church family five nights a week in London. Yet when they move to another country, they stop going to church or only do so half-heartedly. What has happened? He now wonders if this group spends an unsustainable amount of time in church activity without having fundamentally rested in Jesus.

Another common danger with "church time" is not a failure to give it, but a failure to use it wisely. The biblical picture of church being a family is a beautiful one—but we are to be an outward-looking and growing family. The church is not meant to be a family where people simply spend time with one another without any aspiration to grow in maturity or reach out to share the gospel. If we are going to church to sit in a "holy huddle" where things are easy or comfortable and risk-free, then we're going to church to worship the idol of "an easy life".

A cousin of this is to use church to worship the idol of escapism. Some people can spend time at church, hang around chatting after meetings and sign up for things every night of the week... because it has become an excuse for avoiding other responsibilities. Sometimes family relationships are tough or work is tough, and you receive more respect at church than at home or at the factory, so it's easy to overly commit in the arena where you feel most rewarded. When we say "yes" to doing something at church, then, just as much as when we say "no", we should ask: *What is my motive for answering this way?* A "yes" or a "no" are not in themselves right or wrong—it's motive that matters.

USING OUR GIFTS

The Lord Jesus has given us time and abilities to use for him—and so, unsurprisingly, he asks and expects us to use them for his people, the church:

> Each of you should use whatever gift you have received
> to serve others, as faithful stewards of God's grace in its
> various forms. (1 Peter 4 v 10)

Peter tells us that we are "stewards" of the time and gifts that Jesus has lent us. They actually belong to him and he wants us to use them to serve others. If we are not using our gifts to serve people at church in some way, then we are probably falling below the line of obedience. Church is not a hotel, where someone makes your bed, cooks your food and cleans up after you. It's more like a family camping trip, where everyone needs to pitch in. In my experience, it takes multiple people to get the tent up straight. Someone cooks, another clears up, and even the youngest family members are given some little jobs to do. So, just check your view of church— hotel or a family camping trip?

Just occasionally someone will say to me: "I don't know what my role is at church". My response? "Thank you for letting me know! Make a start by considering who you can encourage and how—all of us should be about that. Then let's have a chat about what needs doing at church and what's the best way for you to serve."

In this, as in so many areas we're thinking about, there are different seasons of life, different circumstances within life, and great freedom between reaching obedience and tipping into idolatry. For example, one medic at our church placed his career on pause for four years while he spent lots of time initiating and then growing a ministry to international students. He knowingly turned down the opportunity for promotion and sat on the same pay grade for several years as it meant he had more time to invest in growing the ministry. After four years he decided that he needed to step back from the international work in order to move on in his career. It was an unusual decision he took, to place his career on pause, but one that has borne great gospel fruit. No one is obliged to copy him, but in eternity, I think he'll be delighted with the decision he made.

The Lord has left us with an enormous amount of freedom in how much "church activity" we undertake. It may well be that you could read the Bible one to one with someone this year, but next year that's going to be impossible. You may have led a homegroup for the last couple of years, but with a new baby on the way and an awkward scenario at work it may be sensible to step back for a few months. You may have recently retired, and now you can step up and spend time serving your church in all kinds of ways. You may have annual leave that you could use to help out on a Christian youth summer camp.

What about you? With the reckless freedom of a stranger, let me ask:

- *Do you ever invite people at church to suggest how best you could be serving?*
- *Are you perhaps sitting on the fringes of church or stuck in a bit of a rut?*
- *Do you need to change your view of weekends, to make meeting with church a fairly immovable rock rather than the first thing to give up?*
- *As you read the third column on our chart, does something need to change in order for you to be wholehearted when it comes to church?*

I would expect there to be some reading this who are conscious of letting time run through their fingers and know that they could probably plan their schedules more usefully. Others feel constantly stretched and overcommitted. Perhaps a large number of us are conscious of both. We fritter time away on silly things and then feel constantly overstretched!

Yet before we try to draw up some resolutions in regard to time, let's take one more area. What about down time? How should we think about leisure or just a good old "veg-out" on the sofa?

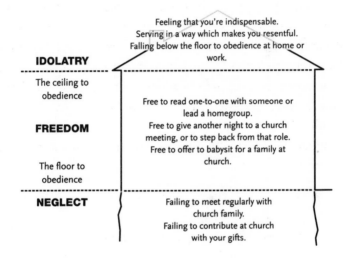

IDOLATRY

Feeling that you're indispensable.
Serving in a way which makes you resentful.
Falling below the floor to obedience at home or work.

The ceiling to obedience

FREEDOM

Free to read one-to-one with someone or lead a homegroup.
Free to give another night to a church meeting, or to step back from that role.
Free to offer to babysit for a family at church.

The floor to obedience

NEGLECT

Failing to meet regularly with church family.
Failing to contribute at church with your gifts.

10. TIME FOR LEISURE

We need to think about having a break. We need to get serious about being playful.

Where does time off fit into a Christian view of time? We've said that going to bed is one essential part of trusting the Lord, but what about relaxing and holidays? Also, what about chores? Work, family and church may take up a good chunk of our time but when do I clean the bathroom, iron my shirts and wash my underwear?

THE REQUIREMENT TO REST

I can't see that leisure is ever commanded in the Bible, but time off to recuperate certainly is. We said back in chapter three that the biblical command to rest is fundamentally a command to place your faith in Jesus. But this doesn't mean that physical rest is unimportant. We remain creatures made from dust, frail and dependent upon God. We still need sleep and we still need time off from labour. Whatever your views on the Sabbath, it seems that the rhythm of six days of work and one day of rest is built into the creation in Genesis 1, and if we reject that for too long, then we'll burn out.

Sensible parents place sweets out of reach of their toddlers. Parents know that left on their own, a small child will greedily snatch every sweet possible and then, after a short delay, be horribly sick. In his kindness God gave the Sabbath to his people in the Old Testament to stop them greedily snatching at every hour in the week to work. If we do that, we'll become sick.

When God insists upon this in Deuteronomy 5, he makes it clear that working seven days a week is slavery:

> [12] Observe the Sabbath day by keeping it holy, as the LORD your God has commanded you. [13] Six days you shall labour and do all your work, [14] but the seventh day is a sabbath to the LORD your God. On it you shall not do any work, neither you, nor your son or daughter, nor your male or female servant, nor your ox, your donkey or any of your animals, nor any foreigner residing in your towns, so that your male and female servants may rest, as you do. [15] Remember that you were slaves in Egypt and that the LORD your God brought you out of there with a mighty hand and an outstretched arm. Therefore the LORD your God has commanded you to observe the Sabbath day. (Deuteronomy 5 v 12-15)

As the Israelites are no longer slaves in Egypt, they should not live as though they are slaves to their work. This would have been particularly challenging at harvest time. You can imagine Farmer Israelite thinking: *The Sabbath is all well and good, but God wouldn't have meant us to keep it during harvest. We need to collect the crops before any damage is done to them.* And God knew the temptation to overwork would be at its strongest during harvest time, so he kindly made his will explicit:

> Six days you shall labour, but on the seventh day you
> shall rest; even during the ploughing season and harvest
> you must rest. (Exodus 34 v 21)

Personally, I'm not persuaded that the Sabbath is binding for Christians in the same way it was for Israel. If you are, then you should keep it. But what is certain is that we are foolish if we ignore the rhythms that God has built into creation. Consistently failing to take one day off a week from your paid work suggests an idolatrous obsession with that work.

Alongside this weekly event, God also included three festivals of thanksgiving into the rhythm of the year. The people were to gather and make offerings of thanks to the Lord (Exodus 23 v 14-19). They were to enjoy themselves with a good meal and good drink (Deuteronomy 14 v 22-27).

There are no comparable instructions for Christians in the New Testament. Yet we are still humans who need rest from our physical labours and who need to pause and deliberately give thanks for God's blessings to us. Perhaps the New Testament emphasis on self-denial, on duty and on seriousness in living the Christian life can lead some of us to feel guilty about taking and appreciating time to relax and enjoy the world around us. We shouldn't. We were built to need it.

THE GIFT OF LEISURE

So, even if there's no explicit comment on leisure, the Bible does require time away from work, whatever "work" looks like for each of us. We're to spend time taking pleasure in God's creation: to pause and to appreciate and give thanks for what God has given us. The Lord has not merely made a functional world for us to work in. He has made a beautiful world for us to enjoy.

He has made trees that are pleasing to the eye and given us light that is sweet to the eye (Genesis 2 v 9; Ecclesiastes 11 v 7). He gave us wine to gladden our hearts and oil to make our faces shine (Psalm 104 v 15). There is a playfulness to God's creation. He made wild beasts to play in the hills; he made the seas teem with a variety of creatures, and the leviathan to frolic in the ocean (Job 40 v 20; Psalm 104 v 25-26). And to reject this is anti-Christian. Paul warns Timothy that forbidding people to enjoy certain foods or enjoy marriage is demonic, because God created good things to be received with thanksgiving (1 Timothy 4 v 1-4). We are to enjoy the world that he has given us to live in. Psalm 104 is a lovely picture of life in God's world. Humanity goes to work in the morning and comes home in the evening. Yet we are to meditate upon God's creation and enjoy the sheer abundance of creatures he has made. We are meant not just to "work" or "not work", but to stop, enjoy and appreciate.

There have been times when I have got this wrong. At certain periods of life I have viewed time away from work as having only one purpose: to refresh me for more work. No doubt many employers would be happy if we thought that way! Yet the idea that time off is purely in order to make us more productive in work is not biblical—it's quasi-Marxist and it's dehumanising. It reduces us to mere economic units, rather than men and women made in God's image to rule and enjoy the world under him.

Some of us find this hard. We find relaxing difficult. Jobs are demanding and so when we do have time off it can take a long time to "wind down". (Amazing, isn't it, how clock language has infected even our leisure time.) I have irritated my family in the past by being relentless in supposed leisure time. I used to get annoyed if I didn't manage to read at least three books during a week's holiday. Sometimes, I ended up reading through the night in order to hit my quota. I would finish holidays with no more sleep in the bank then when I began. That's daft. What does it matter how many books get read? I've (just about) learned that my family and I are happier if I don't import quotas and deadlines from work time into time off! We need to rest in a restful way.

I also find that I can go through the motions of leisure but still be obsessed with something at work or in the family. I might go for a run but spend all of it thinking about a tricky individual. I might sit in the same room as my family, yet have my mind whirring elsewhere.

Equally, just because you're not at work or church or with your family doesn't mean you're enjoying leisure time! The UK government estimates that time spent on the "unpaid economy" is worth £97 billion per year. The unpaid economy is what we might call "running the home"—unpaid childcare, cooking, cleaning, laundry, care of elderly parents and so on. None of these fit into our three arenas so far. All of them are time consuming.

And then there are other activities which are hard to categorise. Is gardening at home restful or just another job that needs to get done? What about cooking? Some people find these relaxing; for others they're a burden.

It might be useful to think of such activities along a spectrum (adapted from Leland Ryken's *Redeeming the Time*, page 43):

PAID WORK		UNPAID WORK		POSSIBLE LEISURE		ABSOLUTE LEISURE
Our employment	>	Ironing Home admin Childcare	>	Cooking Gardening Decorating	>	Reading a book Playing sport Going to the theatre

So it is helpful to ask yourself: *What do I find genuinely refreshing?* It may be that two years ago, baking a cake was relaxing as you only did it occasionally, but now, for whatever reason, you bake twice a week, and it's more a chore than a rest.

If we never have any time when we can sit back and give unrushed thanks for the pleasures of this world, then we're probably neglecting God's purposes for our mental and physical rest. Isn't it great that there are times when obeying God means stopping, resting, and relaxing?!

THE IDOLATRY OF LEISURE

It's much easier to see how leisure can become an idol. Although Paul cautions Timothy against those who condemn healthy pleasures (1 Timothy 4 v 1-3), he warns at greater length about people who are "lovers of pleasure rather than lovers of God" (2 Timothy 3 v 4).

In our modern culture, there are more ways of entertaining ourselves than ever. Sometimes idolatry in this area is easy to spot. Occasionally I go and watch Chelsea Football Club play. There is always one banner displayed declaring proudly: *Chelsea is our religion. Jose* [Mourinho, the manager] *is our God.* All around, men who would see singing in church as girly are pouring out their praises to their team. Their money has been spent on having a seat in the cathedral; their mood for the next few days will be influenced mainly by how well eleven men in blue shirts play; their anger will be directed at anyone who gets in the way of victory. Let's call this for what it is: it's idolatry.

Sporting pursuits can be a wonderful way of relaxing. For those in office jobs where they are bent over a desk for most of the day, some physical activity is important. A morning spent playing golf, cycling or on the cricket pitch can be a blissful way of relaxing (as long as the rest of your family don't mind). A competitive team sport played weekly can be physically and relationally very satisfying.

Yet the good pleasure that is sport can quickly drift into an obsession. I think that people used to go to the gym to exercise; now they "work out". People used to play tennis; now they "work on their backhand". This may all be innocent, but it reveals a certain drivenness in our leisure pursuits that may mean that we're not actually relaxing. We don't feel we can simply rest and enjoy ourselves; there has to be an outcome, a measure of productivity.

As with other areas of life, it's impossible to prescribe here. Many of my peers now spend time training for triathlons. I would love to do so. It would be good for me (and my girth). Yet I don't think my family can cope with the extra time that it would take to get fit enough to complete one. Not at the moment. In a few years? Maybe.

Travel can be great. Yet it can lead to an obsession with gathering stamps in a passport and photos on Instagram. For many, accumulation of experiences has replaced accumulation of physical stuff. It seems to me that, as rising property prices have made buying a house or flat increasingly unlikely, people have replaced that ambition with the desire to own experiences. You haven't lived if your Facebook page isn't full of photos from your time on other continents. Equally, at the other end of life, it is worth asking what retirement is for. It might be a real blessing to you and your church family if you use the time well. But if early retirement is simply to play golf or travel the world, is that really a sensible way to use the time the Lord has given you?

THE BLESSING OF FRIENDSHIP

Friendship is something that generally takes place in leisure time. Hopefully we have friends at church; possibly we have them at work. Yet good friendships need to be intentionally pursued. If we have no good friends that we see or at least speak to regularly, that may function as a warning light that we need to carve out more time off. In the book of Proverbs, friendship is repeatedly commended as a key factor in shaping who we are and bringing delight. For instance:

> Perfume and incense bring joy to the heart, and the pleasantness of a friend springs from their heartfelt advice. (27 v 9)

It's incredibly easy for friendships to get pushed to the bottom of our mental to-do lists—perhaps particularly if you're a guy. There are no deadlines in friendship and so it's easy to let them drift. This can be exacerbated sometimes by the illusion of friendship that social media can create. We may have many "friends" on Facebook, yet no one to truly turn to for honest counsel, practical support and physical engagement. Put starkly, some of us need to get out of cyberspace and spend more time face to face.

The busyness of life can easily squeeze out friendships and yet they are such a precious gift. As C. S. Lewis observed:

> *Friendship has no survival value but it's one of the things that gives value to survival.*

As a church pastor, I go to plenty of weddings and have heard hundreds of wedding speeches. Undoubtedly one of the nicest comments I've heard was in a best man's speech a few years ago. After the normal gentle mockery of the groom and an edited history of some of his more embarrassing moments, the best man turned to praise the groom's spiritual qualities. He finished simply by saying:

> *Thank you for having me as your best man. Thank you much more for making me a better man through your Christian friendship.*

Committing to friendships will only make the juggle of time harder. But few things give as much pleasure in this life, or help us grow so much in our character. According to Proverbs, investing in good friendships is the way to walk wisely and avoid ruin (eg: Proverbs 12 v 26; 18 v 24; 22 v 25).

STRIKING A BALANCE

How do you know you're above the floor, but not into idolatry?

Overall, leisure is great. We need time off from work—all kinds of work. We're denying our creatureliness if we don't take time off. Yet we must not become too rigid. Jesus showed us that sometimes the sensible desire for time off and recreation can be sacrificed for a greater good.

> [30] The apostles gathered round Jesus and reported to him all they had done and taught. [31] Then, because so many people were coming and going that they did not even have a chance to eat, he said to them, "Come with me by yourselves to a quiet place and get some rest."
>
> [32] So they went away by themselves in a boat to a solitary place. [33] But many who saw them leaving recognised them and ran on foot from all the towns and got there ahead of them. [34] When Jesus landed and saw a large crowd, he had compassion on them, because they were like sheep without a shepherd. So he began teaching them many things. (Mark 6 v 30-34)

It's such an interesting episode. The apostles were exhausted and needed leisure—and Jesus recognised this as a necessary and good thing: "Come with me by yourselves to a quiet place and get some rest". But then he saw a crowd in need; and leisure time was postponed. We must not ignore our need for down time; nor must we become too precious about it. Sometimes plans get sidelined by the needs of others, and that's entirely right. Equally, those plans should exist in the first place! In Mark 6, rest was not ignored but postponed. Later in the same chapter, Jesus sends the apostles off in a boat on their own, while he takes time to pray (v 45-46). Both spiritual and physical rest can be delayed but they cannot be ignored completely.

So, do play. Do veg out. Do enjoy culture at the Royal Opera House or at the Red Lion pub. Play sport, watch sport, be a good sport. Do it with your family, your church family... and, sometimes, just on your own or with a friend. You know how you relax—what it is that refreshes you. It will be different from those around you. But do make sure you do it. Rest.

To take time to enjoy what God has given in creation is a lovely thing. Taking time to enjoy man's creativity on the sports pitch, in the cinema or in museums is a healthy thing to do.

All this is an important act of faith. It's the demonstration that we are trusting in God to sustain and provide, and to be in control. Leisure is a spiritual activity.

There is probably more freedom here than in any other arena we've looked at because what "leisure" or refreshment is varies so widely from person to person. Adam might find nothing as restful as playing with his daughter. Beth might find writing a Bible study so different from everything else she does that it is uniquely refreshing. Colin might find reading Christian biographies an absolute treat. Yet it's possible to imagine that other people would find all three of these activities draining. Learning what drains us and what refreshes us makes a massive difference to how tired we feel.

So here's how the leisure-time floor and ceiling looks...

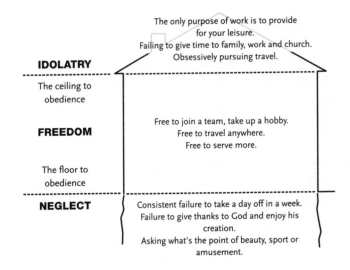

IDOLATRY

The ceiling to obedience

The only purpose of work is to provide for your leisure.
Failing to give time to family, work and church.
Obsessively pursuing travel.

FREEDOM

Free to join a team, take up a hobby.
Free to travel anywhere.
Free to serve more.

The floor to obedience

NEGLECT

Consistent failure to take a day off in a week.
Failure to give thanks to God and enjoy his creation.
Asking what's the point of beauty, sport or amusement.

11. TIME FOR RESOLUTIONS

If you're going to use your time well—if you're going to be busy, but not feel burdened—here's what you need to remember about your time:

It's not yours. It belongs to your Lord.

In *The Screwtape Letters*, C. S. Lewis has the cunning demon Screwtape offer this advice on how to prevent a Christian from being useful:

> *You must therefore zealously guard in his mind the curious assumption "My time is my own". Let him have the feeling that he starts each day as the lawful possessor of twenty-four hours. Let him feel as a grievous tax that portion of this property which he has to make over to his employers, and as a generous donation that further portion which he allows to religious duties. But what he must never be permitted to doubt is that the total from which these deductions have been made was, in some mysterious sense, his own personal birthright.*

If you think your time is your "own personal birthright", it will naturally make you selfish and resentful about anyone or anything that makes demands upon your time—including God. So let's turn this perspective on its head. The fundamental question that all of us need to ask about "our" time is:

What changes should I make in order to maximise my
faithfulness in serving the Lord with the time he has given me?

We have a limited amount of time here on earth, and we need to use it as best we can to grow Jesus' kingdom. Please don't get to the end of this book, put it down, and move on. In this chapter I want to lay down a few final markers.

DO WHAT YOU CAN

Do you feel constantly pulled in too many directions? As though the to-do list is never ending and ever extending? Let me pass on some simple words of Jesus that I've always found encouraging: "Do what you can".

Shortly before his death, Jesus is enjoying dinner with his disciples and friends. And a woman pours a jar of very expensive perfume over Jesus' head. It's an extravagant gesture and it causes outrage among some present, because it could have been sold for a large sum of money to be given to the poor.

Jesus' response is lovely:

"Leave her alone," said Jesus. "Why are you bothering
her? She has done a beautiful thing to me ... She did
what she could. She poured perfume on my body
beforehand to prepare for my burial. Truly I tell you,
wherever the gospel is preached throughout the world,
what she has done will also be told, in memory of her."

(Mark 14 v 6, 8-9)

I know that it was money being spent on Jesus and not time; but the principle remains. This woman gave her most precious possession to Jesus because she loved him. She may not have understood lots; she may not have been able to influence the events that were about to unfold in Jerusalem; there were lots of things she could not do. Yet she did what she could with what she had.

I often look at all I would like to do, add on everything other people want me to do... and groan. And I'm picked up by the simple observation: God wants me to do what I can—and he sees it as beautiful when I do. He knows that I'm limited and unable to do all that I desire. He does want the best of me and from me—but he does not seek more than that. So I do what I can.

The other striking thing about the woman's sacrifice is that it will be remembered for ever, Jesus says. When the gospel of Jesus dying for sins is re-told, we remember her sacrifice for that cause. How encouraging that the sacrifices we make for Jesus are remembered!

Remember, Jesus was overwhelmed by the crowds wanting him (Mark 3 v 7-10). He didn't always get rest when he wanted it (Mark 6 v 31-33). He didn't heal every sick person in Palestine; he walked away from some (Luke 4 v 43). He didn't do *every* thing. He said "no" to good things so that he could do the most important thing. He finished the work that God the Father gave him to do. So can you and I.

Some of us need to make changes to our lives so that we are living sustainably, rather than just surviving from year to year. Some of us need to make changes so that we are living sacrificially, rather than just cruising through. Some of us will need to do both, in different areas of life.

But there is not time for *every* thing. Recognise that. There is time for *every thing God asks of us*. Recognise that too. We do what we can.

And to help you do that, I'd encourage you to be two things: reliable, and deliberate.

BE DELIBERATE

Jesus was very clear on his priorities. That's why he was able to choose to say "yes" to his preaching ministry and "no" to healing ministry when it would have prevented him preaching (Luke 4 v 42-44). Being clear on what matters will prevent us from being fickle or being driven into decisions by guilt.

BE RELIABLE

Ours is a flighty culture that often drops commitments at a whim. Christians are to be reliable. If we say we'll do something, we'll do it. If we commit to give time to something, then we should honour our commitments. Too often people seem to change their minds because a better offer comes along, or they don't feel like it any more. Honouring our promises can also stop us feeling harassed as we're pulled from one thing to the next.

Perhaps we need to learn to apply Paul's instruction to the Corinthian church to our own culture and lives:

> Each person should remain in the situation they were in
> when God called them.   (1 Corinthians 7 v 20)

Paul may well say to us in the modern West: *Yes, change jobs and move houses—that's all fine. But that stuff is a lot less important than you think. This world is passing away. What's most important is that you are constant in serving the Lord. Often, you'll be of most use serving him if you stay in one job, one church or one neighbourhood for as long as possible.*

With that in mind, let's look at our completed "time-table":

	WORK	HOME	CHURCH	LEISURE
IDOLATRY The ceiling to obedience	Working primarily for the boss, not the Lord. Consistently working 7 days a week, and not resting. Working primarily for meaning, envy, greed or anxiety. Falling below the floor to obedience at church or at home.	Loving parents or children more than Jesus (Matthew 10 v 37). Skipping church regularly to take kids to a sports game. Falling below the floor to obedience at church or at work.	Feeling that you're indispensable. Serving in a way which makes you resentful. Falling below the floor to obedience at work or at home.	The only purpose of work is to provide for your leisure. Falling below the floor to obedience at church, at home or at work. Obsessively pursuing travel.
FREEDOM	Working for the Lord.	Free to go on a romantic weekend away or not. Free to take the family on holiday or not. Free to go to the football game or not.	Free to read one-to-one with someone or lead a homegroup Free to give another night to a church meeting or to step back from that role. Free to offer to babysit for a family at church.	Free to join a team, or take up a hobby. Free to travel anywhere. Free to serve more.
The floor to obedience				
NEGLECT	Failure to provide for yourself and have something to share (Ephesians 4 v 28). Only working hard when the boss has his eye on you (Ephesians 6 v 6).	Putting your own self interest and comfort above family. Failing to teach Christ and model love of him above all else. Breaking promises of time with your children. Neglecting your parents.	Failing to meet regularly with church family. Failing to contribute at church with your gifts.	Consistent failure to take a day off in a week. Failure to give thanks to God and enjoy his creation. Asking what's the point of beauty sport or amusement.

WORKING IT THROUGH

I want to run through a number of examples of how real people I know have chosen to use all that freedom between neglect and idolatry. I'm not commenting on whether I think they've made good or bad decisions; their decisions may be useful as comparisons and to fuel your own thinking. I do want to stress again that there is freedom. None of the examples I'm giving here are prescriptive. None of the questions that I ask have one answer to them. They are merely here to provoke thought.

Beth is 28 years old, single and works for a consultancy firm that typically works with one client for six months. She loves the work and the firm. She has enjoyed the excitement of working with lots of bright people in a small firm that is expanding rapidly. Her hours are normally manageable for the first four months of a project, but in the last six to eight weeks she can work up to 80 hours a week and will often miss church on a Sunday in order to fly to somewhere in Europe. At the end of her last project she recognised that this was not really sustainable and so told her boss that she was willing to work long hours Monday to Friday but was not willing to lose her weekends. Her boss agreed and so she is happily staying at her firm. She is able to plug in and serve on Sundays at church as well as catch up with friends in a manner she thinks is sustainable.

- *Are you bold enough to have a similar conversation with your boss?*

Paul is a salesman for a double-glazing company. He's pretty good at the job but, having done it for years, is frankly a little bored. Lots of people have told him he should do something more challenging. However, he normally replies that being satisfied in his job is a secondary consideration. What matters most is his Christian life. Currently, he can get home at 5:30pm and have lots of time with the kids. He also has plenty of time to serve at church, which he does by leading in evangelism, and by going and visiting people from church at home in order to encourage them.

- *Would you be willing to do a job that you find a bit dull in order to maximise the time you have for Christian ministry?*

Nicola is a schoolteacher in a busy school. During term time she admits that she "enters the tunnel of work and Christian ministry at work", and then emerges to her family's delight during the holidays when she has plenty of time to spend with them. She and her husband have accepted a certain boom-and-bust cycle to their year. As long as extra-curricular work trips don't eat into holidays, all is well with her being consumed by work during term. She gets great unrushed time with the family during holidays.

- *Do you consider the balance of a year? Times of high emotional energy and draining work are fine as long as they are compensated for by periods of low stress and demand. It's when there's no ebb and flow that your health and other relationships suffer.*

David is married with three teenage children. His work requires him to travel overseas for a few days most weeks, either to Europe or the States. I asked him how he managed to juggle all his commitments and he told me his "golden rules":

1. He had to have his wife's approval before taking a job or moving to a new role in the firm.

2. Wherever he was in the world, he daily found a time to have either a telephone conversation or Skype conversation with his wife and the kids. He would curtail meetings at work in order to make that time every day.

3. He would never miss church on a Sunday morning and so often flew out of the UK at bizarre times; and as far as is humanly possible, he would not miss the monthly prayer meeting.

Bear in mind that his kids are of an age where they can have decent conversations on the telephone, rather than monosyllabic grunts. He couldn't have done this a few years ago.

- *If you're married, have both of you signed up for a certain pattern of work, or is one growing deeply frustrated?*

John is a painter-decorator. He was formerly a pastor and he still loves preaching. However, one of his children is disabled and their care costs are very high and not all covered by the state. He and his wife took the decision that she could earn more than him as a schoolteacher and so provide financially for the family. He became a painter-decorator because it's extremely flexible time-wise and means that he can drop things quite easily to care for his daughter in an emergency. However, most school holidays he takes a week or two out for intensive preaching trips.

- *Could you still joyfully serve the Lord if you were no longer able to do the job you love?*

Josh and Karen are a married couple who were both working in demanding law firms. They found that by the time they got to the weekend they were both exhausted. They spent much of Saturday doing chores such as shopping, and then a good chunk of Sunday with people from church. They became conscious that their time with one another was often poor and was spent collapsed in front of the TV. They were involved at church but they had little to give and were a little resentful of the time it took. They therefore both decided to ask their respective firms to let them work a four-day week. They were told that this would not help their promotion prospects, and obviously it involved a pay cut but they accepted that trade-off. The reality is that they sometimes still work five days a week but those are eight-hour days as opposed to ten-hour days. They see more of one another and have more energy for friends and family.

- *Would you ask the question that they asked, in order to have a sustainable pattern?*

Charis had been very successful in a job that she enjoyed. Now with children in school, she works three days a week in a dull job. She runs a Bible-study group for women and helps out at a mums-and-tots group. The income is necessary to help pay the mortgage on their house but she finds the part-time work less fulfilling than her previous full-time work, and she certainly feels that she has less status. She was very tempted to apply for another full-time job but thinks that, on balance, her work leading Bible studies and helping at church would suffer too much.

- *Do you view all your roles in life as God-given? Worker, parent, spouse and neighbour could all be viewed as "callings". It's unlikely that all are equally stimulating. We need to "do what we can" to honour the Lord in all of them.*

Matt (yes, this one is me) recently came out of footballing retirement to join a six-a-side football team of local dads. Every Tuesday night I was re-living the dream. No matter that the combined age of our team was a massive 272 years. Nor that twenty-somethings beat us soundly most weeks (note though, most, not all). Yet after a few weeks my wife pointed out that, alongside weekly church commitments, I was therefore out four or five nights a week. "Perhaps that's a little unfair on me and the family?" she suggested. Fair point. It was great fun, good exercise and beginning to have some gospel use to it. However, it was just too much at the moment.

- *First question: What was I thinking, trying to play football?!*
- *Second (more serious) question: Does your leisure time also work for the rest of your family—spouse, children, and parents?*

Nicki is a single woman in her late forties who is extremely competent at her job. She is also a stalwart of the church, and her parents expect more visits from her than from her married brother. She has recently dropped down to four days a week and is in the privileged position of being able to afford to. She wanted to spend time on different things. She wanted to have lunch with friends—perhaps go to the cinema. She wanted more time to prepare Bible studies or meet one to one with someone. She had reached a point of resenting the treadmill of work, yet recognised that she needs to be in employment for another 15 to 20 years. Now she feels in a more sustainable pattern and has got a little bit of slack to take up a new challenge and to honour her parents.

- *Is it possible to make relatively small changes to your routine that could help you serve Christ and break a seeming monotony?*

Andrew is in the privileged position of being a consultant doctor with some say in his shift patterns. He has completely blocked out Wednesday afternoons in order to pick his kids up from school, give them dinner and chat. He thinks that the time he has doing this without Mummy around means the children relate to him differently then. Okay, not all of us have that freedom with our hours, but it comes at a cost of income to him. That's one session in the week where he could be making money but he's decided not to.

- *Is it feasible to take a salary cut for an "hours-cut"?*

Ben is on the road quite a bit with work. He decided, with his wife, to set an upper limit to nights away from home. That number has ebbed and flowed depending upon the kids' ages but he has been proactive in setting a number and manoeuvring at work to keep to it. As he puts it simply, you cannot have the same rules when your kids are pre-school as when they have flown the nest. It's better to have agreed a set number of nights away than have resentment slowly growing.

- *Would setting quotas with your family to certain activities in your work or life help?*

Giles found that the demands of his job meant that he could rarely ever make his mid-week fellowship group at church. After a while he realised he was not alone in this and so assembled a group that now always meets on a Sunday before church. He now feels encouraged and less guilty about letting other people down. In admitting defeat, he came up with a completely new scenario!

- *Can you simply move some events around in the week?*

PROACTIVE PLANNING

You have to make time to work out how best to use your time; and you need to do it regularly. An annual "state of the nation" is a sensible thing to do, because commitments will vary over time, as will your own capacity.

This is also something that is much easier to do with someone else. Who is there that can honestly help you assess your choices and commitments? You need some people who understand the multiple claims upon your time, and who are also wanting to maximise their own usefulness to Jesus.

For married couples, the back half of a holiday is often a good time to take stock. When you've relaxed and are not irritated with one another, discussions tend to be more reasonable. Yet if there are big decisions to be made, don't make them simply inside your marriage. Often the outside perspective of people you trust is enormously helpful.

For those who are single, the counsel of prayer-triplet partners or good Christian friends, combined with the advice of a godly older Christian brother or sister, is priceless. When there is no one under the same roof suggesting to you that life is out of kilter, you do need to be honest with others if their counsel is to be of any use.

The important things are to choose how you spend the time, rather than being always at the mercy of events; to be liberated to say "no" as well as "yes"; to be obedient in all the circumstances God has called you to, and to avoid turning any of those gifts into idols.

Taking a step back and analysing *why* we are pulled around so much by the demands on our time is crucial. But when you do this, don't forget to ask the bigger questions that make sure you're not wasting time on the wrong things. The reality of eternity must shape our life here and now as much as the ticking clock does. So be asking:

- *Am I using my time and gifts to grow the kingdom of Jesus?*
- *When I'm retired and sit in my rocking chair, what will I be most delighted that I gave my time to?*

All our time belongs to the Lord. He doesn't ask us to do *every* thing; but he does call us to do what we can. And when we do, he says: *They have done a beautiful thing.*

Whenever we draw breath as a couple or a family and have a "state of the nation" conversation about how we're using our time, we begin with the wonderful closing words of Psalm 90 v 17:

> May the favour of the Lord our God rest on us;
> establish the work of our hands for us—
> yes, establish the work of our hands.

12. TIME FOR BED

*If I could hear Christ praying in the next room, I would not
fear a million enemies.*   *Robert Murray McCheyne*

Some people are only just waking up to how good sleep is.

Claire Danes is the American star of the TV series
Homeland, where her character, Carrie, is in permanent need
of a psychiatrist. She recently told *Vogue* magazine:

> *I'm from the land of therapy, and I love it but Hugh [her
> English husband] really helped me to discover that a lot of
> the time, I'm just tired.*

She's just saved herself a lot of money and a lot of time on a
therapist's couch! Take a nap and feel better.

Getting into bed and going to sleep is a wonderful thing.
The problem is that these days, there are so many other
things to do in bed: watch TV, do the grocery shopping
online, and send emails. I want to finish this book about
time with a brief reminder of God's sovereignty and so the
encouragement: *Go to sleep*. Do what you can in the day,

and trust that God will do what he does at night.

Let's look at two psalms. Read through them slowly, drinking in each verse, seeing what it tells you about the writer, and (more importantly) about God and our relationship with him as his people:

Psalm 3
A psalm of David. When he fled from his son Absalom.

¹ LORD, how many are my foes!
　　How many rise up against me!
² Many are saying of me,
　　"God will not deliver him."
³ But you, LORD, are a shield around me,
　　my glory, the One who lifts my head high.
⁴ I call out to the LORD,
　　and he answers me from his holy mountain.
⁵ I lie down and sleep;
　　I wake again, because the LORD sustains me.
⁶ I will not fear though tens of thousands
　　assail me on every side.
⁷ Arise, LORD! Deliver me, my God!
Strike all my enemies on the jaw;
　　break the teeth of the wicked.
⁸ From the LORD comes deliverance.
　　May your blessing be on your people.

Psalm 121
¹ I lift up my eyes to the mountains—
　　where does my help come from?
² My help comes from the LORD,
　　the Maker of heaven and earth.
³ He will not let your foot slip—
　　he who watches over you will not slumber;

4 indeed, he who watches over Israel
    will neither slumber nor sleep.
5 The LORD watches over you—
    the LORD is your shade at your right hand;
6 the sun will not harm you by day,
    nor the moon by night.
7 The LORD will keep you from all harm—
    he will watch over your life;
8 the LORD will watch over your coming and going
    both now and for evermore.

In Psalm 3, David is stressed, and with very good reason! His son, Absalom, has deposed him as king, and David is fleeing for his life. But by the second half of the psalm, he's able to go to sleep (v 5)! Why? The movement through his song is from the fear of abandonment in verses 1-2, through a reflection upon God's revealed character in verse 3, to the confidence that grows in verses 4-8. David lies down and sleeps because he knows the One who protects him.

David can go to sleep because he trusts the LORD, who never sleeps. Psalm 121 beautifully describes our un-sleeping God. The one who "will neither slumber nor sleep" will not allow us to slip dangerously, or be harmed irrevocably. That's true of every individual believer (v 3), and true of his people as a whole (v 4). It's true in the immediate circumstances that trouble us (v 5-6). It's true in the whole of our lives (v 7-8).

David sleeps because he knows that the LORD does not slumber or sleep. Here he reveals in embryo the trust that his greater descendant, Jesus, shows in his Father—the confidence which said, as he hung on his cross: "Father, into your hands I commit my spirit" (Luke 23 v 46).

David could go to sleep despite having lost his kingdom due to one of his own family deposing him. He nodded off even though he feared for his life and the lives of other family members back in Jerusalem. If David could go to sleep in the middle of this, then surely you can go to sleep, whatever you are facing. Knowing that the LORD is watching over us is a simple truth that can prevent a young child's nightmares, but also calm the fears of a king.

We can trust that the LORD watches over us. We should work hard during the day to achieve as much as we can; but we should stop work at night and trust the Lord for the outcomes of life.

TRUSTING HIS TIMING

Right at the beginning of this book, we saw that "there is a time for everything" (Ecclesiastes 3 v 1). There are times and seasons that we would not choose—events that we do not desire, and challenges that we do not want to face. And they may well last for longer than we want. Joseph was imprisoned for at least two years and did not see his father for thirteen. David waited fifteen years between being chosen as king and being crowned, most of them spent on the run. But Joseph and David did not stop trusting God; they used the time he'd given them, in the places he'd put them, for the period he'd placed them there.

This is always a time for trusting God, and serving God. After all, he's in charge of it:

> Now listen, you who say, "Today or tomorrow we will go to this or that city, spend a year there, carry on business and make money." Why, you do not even know what will happen tomorrow. What is your life? You are a mist that appears for a little while and then vanishes. Instead, you ought to say, "If it is the Lord's will, we will live and do this or that." (James 4 v 13-15)

We must do all that we can to make the best use of our brief time here on earth. But we do it trusting in him, serving him and following him, and looking forward to being with him.

At the end of a book designed to help you think through how best to use your time for the Lord—how to be busy in life, but not burdened by life—it's time to give thanks for the rest you enjoy in Jesus, even when you're busy... to give thanks that he is watching over you, even as you sleep... and to ask for his help to know what he is calling you to do, and not to do, today and tomorrow.

It's time to pray...

... and then it's time for bed.

THANK YOU...

... to those who read through a draft of this book, when your time is so scarce. Thanks to Hugh, Jody, Marc, Fred, Andre, Vicky and Sharon.

... to my editor, Carl Laferton, who would want me to say to his boss that he is worth every penny for his work (and I would want to say that anyway).

... to Ceri, my wife, who creates time for me, supports my use of time, and is a great example of using time and talents to serve the Lord.

LIVEDIFFERENT

TIMOTHY LANE

LIVING WITHOUT WORRY

If you ever worry, and would love to worry less, this book is for you. You will not find trite, easy answers; but you will find real ones, as you discover what worry is, why you feel it, and how you can replace it with an experience of real, lasting peace in all the ups and downs of your life.

An accessible must-read for anyone who wants to begin the journey of worrying less.

HELEN THORNE, TRAINING MANAGER AT LONDON CITY MISSION

HONEST EVANGELISM

How to talk about Jesus even when it's tough

Rico Tice

YOU CAN REALLY GROW

How to thrive in your Christian life

John Hindley

SERVING WITHOUT SINKING

How to serve Christ and keep your joy

John Hindley

thegoodbook
COMPANY
Opening up the Bible

At The Good Book Company, we are dedicated to helping Christians and local churches grow. We believe that God's growth process always starts with hearing clearly what he has said to us through his timeless word—the Bible.

Ever since we opened our doors in 1991, we have been striving to produce resources that honour God in the way the Bible is used. We have grown to become an international provider of user-friendly resources to the Christian community, with believers of all backgrounds and denominations using our Bible studies, books, evangelistic resources, DVD-based courses and training events.

We want to equip ordinary Christians to live for Christ day by day, and churches to grow in their knowledge of God, their love for one another, and the effectiveness of their outreach.

Call us for a discussion of your needs or visit one of our local websites for more information on the resources and services we provide.

Your friends at The Good Book Company

UK & EUROPE
NORTH AMERICA
AUSTRALIA
NEW ZEALAND

 thegoodbook.co.uk
thegoodbook.com
thegoodbook.com.au
thegoodbook.co.nz

 0333 123 0880
866 244 2165
(02) 6100 4211
(+64) 3 343 2463

 WWW.CHRISTIANITYEXPLORED.ORG
Our partner site is a great place for those exploring the Christian faith, with a clear explanation of the good news, powerful testimonies and answers to difficult questions.